Women of the Vine

Women of the Vine

INSIDE THE WORLD OF WOMEN WHO MAKE, TASTE, AND ENJOY WINE

DEBORAH BRENNER

Foreword by Gina Gallo

JOHN WILEY & SONS, INC.

Published by John Wiley & Sons, Inc., Hoboken, New Jersey
Published simultaneously in Canada

Design and production by Navta Associates, Inc.

Illustration credits: page 8, image courtesy of Deborah Brenner; page 29, courtesy of Handley Cellars; page 41, courtesy of James Fountain; page 49, courtesy of Amelia Ceja; page 59, photograph by John McJunkin, copyright © Andrea Robinson; pages 71 and 133 courtesy of E&J Gallo Winery; page 81, courtesy of Marketta Fourmeaux; page 93, courtesy of Heidi Peterson Barrett; pages 105 and 108, courtesy of Tanit Photography; page 113, photograph by Ben Miller; page 125, courtesy of Markham Vineyards; page 143, photograph by David Ditta; page 151, for A. C. Noble, University of California, Davis, Department of V&E; page 161, photograph by Meg Smith, copyright © 2001; page 175, courtesy of Central Coast Adworks; page 183, courtesy of *Wine Adventure* magazine; page 191, courtesy of Far Niente; page 199, courtesy of KQED Television; page 207, courtesy of Nickel & Nickel; page 217, courtesy of Cathy Gritzseld

For general information about our other products and services, please contact our Customer Care Department within the United States at (800) 762-2974, outside the United States at (317) 572-3993 or fax (317) 572-4002.

Wiley also publishes its books in a variety of electronic formats. Some content that appears in print may not be available in electronic books. For more information about Wiley products, visit our web site at www.wiley.com.

Library of Congress Cataloging-in-Publication Data:

Brenner, Deborah, date.
    Women of the vine : inside the world of women who make, taste, and enjoy wine / Deborah Brenner ; foreword by Gina Gallo.
        p. cm.
    Includes index.
    ISBN-13 978-0-470-09531-7 (cloth : alk.paper)
    ISBN-10 0-470-09531-8 (cloth : alk.paper)
    ISBN-13 978-0-470-06801-4 (pbk. : alk.paper)
    ISBN-10 0-470-06801-9 (pbk. : alk.paper)
 1. Vintners. 2. Women vintners. 3. Wine and wine making. I. Title.
    TP547.A1B74 2006
    641.2'20922—dc22   2006025186

Printed in the United States of America

10 9 8 7 6 5 4 3 2 1

CONTENTS

FOREWORD

BY GINA GALLO

A wise old observer of the world once said, "Wine is a story that leads everywhere." Deborah Brenner has picked up the story of wine at the start of the twenty-first century and has followed it in two directions. She has looked into our history and traditions. At the same time, she gives us an insight into the future of wine through the words of some of the women who are creating that future with their daily work.

When Debbie called to see whether my cousin Stephanie and I would participate in this project, I asked a lot of questions, since "women in wine" is not a new topic. Her approach was a little different. She has a journalist's urge to understand how things work, a writer's need to tell stories, and a woman's perspective on how the pieces of a life fit together. She would use interviews as her text, a historian's technique for documentation, and pull from those interviews the threads she needed to weave her story.

To enhance the interest in the stories, Debbie adds useful information for readers beginning to explore their own worlds of wine. The result is a tapestry of tales well told, highlighted by suggestions for enjoying wine on your own.

The world of wine is neither a man's world nor a woman's world; the patterns of access or exclusion have followed the local cultural norms or acted as signs of the times as women's roles have waxed and waned. But now, as we enter a true Golden Age for wines, women are increasingly visible as leaders in every aspect of wine-growing and winemaking. Wines have never been better or more accessible as part of a life well lived. On the other side of the equation, more and more women are bringing wine to the table to share with family and friends.

Deborah Brenner's work uncovers some of the personal, family, and business dynamics of today's women in wine, but this is not a book about gender. There was a habit among wine writers some time ago, a habit now in decline, to characterize wines as "feminine" or "masculine," making a modern metaphor out of an antique stereotype. One was elegant and nuanced, the other bold and well structured. There has been a continuing search among marketing people for a "woman's wine." That's not what this book is about, either.

This book is about women who work with the wine, making an endless variety of wines from one good ingredient: grapes. It is about women who have families (or not), who are part farmer, part scientist, part chef, part CEO.

There are lessons in the stories if you look for them. You will find little pleasures here, too. Sit back, pour a glass of wine, and enjoy. Cheers.

Healdsburg, California

ACKNOWLEDGMENTS

Silent gratitude isn't much use to anyone.
—Gladys Bronwyn Stern

Taking the quote above as my cue, I want to thank all the people who worked with me and believed in this project. Like the winemakers in this book, it is quite amazing to see the growth of something beautiful from start to finish. And, just like winemaking, it is a collaborative effort and not only the result of one person's labor.

This is a list, and the order is in no way intended to reflect a status of importance. I think it would be impossible to quantify that in any way.

I would like to thank my parents for teaching me that you can achieve whatever you want, as long as you are willing to work hard for it. I thank them for supporting my decisions to pursue my dreams and, as Milla Handley said in chapter 2, for knowing when to sit back and let me become an individual.

I want to thank my boyfriend, Jack, for encouraging me to pursue my passion in wine (one we share together) and always believing in me. He is my biggest fan and has kept me balanced through some very tough times.

This book wouldn't have been published if it weren't for my friend Sue Blessing—a true blessing indeed. She came into my boyfriend's restaurant one night out of the blue, hoping to catch me for a glass of wine. I had just come back from Napa and Sonoma and was so excited about researching women winemakers. I sat with Sue and told her about my vision. She immediately embraced the idea and helped me to formulate a proposal to take to John Wiley & Sons. With enthusiasm and tenacity, Sue held on to the idea until she found the right person to take on the project.

Kitt Allan and Camille Acker were those people. I met with them at Wiley, and very soon afterward, the real journey began. I thank Kitt for taking a chance on me and seeing my potential. I owe Camille big thanks for all of her patience and for being a mentor in guiding me through the publishing process. I also thank her for her keen insight into my vision and her unwavering belief in the success of this book.

Another very important person who not only helped me work on the book but also became a friend in the process is Amy Zavatto. An accomplished author herself, she was an incredible mentor. She is a great writer, and we have very similar styles, so I was so fortunate to work with her.

Of course, I want to thank all of the Women of the Vine—the winemakers, the sommeliers, the wine writers, and the women in wine whom I have met and interviewed. This is a book about your achievements, and I am pleased to have been your voice in telling your amazing stories. Thank you again for your participation and for sharing your lives with me and with everyone who will read this book. You have inspired me so much.

I would like to offer an extra thank-you to Gina Gallo not only for participating in the book but also for agreeing to write the foreword. Gina and I met while she was in New York for the first annual Gallo Family Vineyards Gold Medal Awards. We talked for a long time about everything imaginable, including wine, charity, surfing, family, travel, and pets. Just as the book reveals in its stories, I immediately connected with Gina, not just because we are the same age but because she is a real person who just so happens to be an incredible winemaker.

I also want to thank my two sisters, Lynn and Karen; my wonderful nieces, Lauren, Melissa, and Anna; and the love of my two cats, who kept me company all day while I wrote. To all my family and friends, your continued love and support mean everything to me.

INTRODUCTION

> If there is a book you really want to read but it hasn't
> been written yet, then you must write it.
> —Toni Morrison

WOMEN OF THE VINE IS THE FIRST BOOK WRITTEN ABOUT women in wine that portrays the women themselves instead of discussing their wine and the industry. It enters into their homes and their cellars. It takes you on a new and different journey to wine country and invites you to enjoy the women's stories and share them with family and friends.

This book is not just for women, but for all people who desire to pursue their dreams, take chances, and create the lives they want to live. However, this book also connects at a very intimate level with the world of wine, but it is not about ratings, scores, competition, techniques, or tasting notes. It is about the true pleasure of wine and what it means to so many of us. I hope you will sip some wine and enjoy being inspired with all of your senses as you meet these amazing Women of the Vine.

The Journey Begins

Not so long ago, during a trip to Napa and Sonoma Valley, I was having lunch with Karen Cakebread and a couple of other friends at

Mustards Grill between the towns of Oakville and Yountville in Napa. It was during that hour, while sipping a Cakebread Cellars sauvignon blanc, that my avocation for wine turned into a new profession, but I didn't know it at the time.

My thirst for knowledge—to understand more about women winemakers and the process of winemaking from their own perspectives—was my driving force to return home to Tappan, New York, and start my own journey into the wine industry.

My research began immediately, and I looked into every available source, but I didn't find any books that allowed me to connect with these women and their wines. Amid the interviews, the press releases, and the wine-tasting notes, I could find the women's wine styles and their techniques, as well as winery information and brief blurbs about having children or not—but nothing of who these women truly were. I could find nothing to help me identify with them. From that point on, I felt compelled to tell their stories and share their secrets with women (and men) worldwide.

Maybe I identified with them because I too began a career at the end of the 1980s and spent twenty-plus years in a male-dominated field. I knew instinctively that there had to be more behind the barrels of wine than just a professional woman who chose this career path, because I knew the struggles, the fears, the disappointments, and the triumphs that I had endured in my career and in my life.

I was also curious whether these women were like me, desperately trying to balance work and life, find my purpose, connect with others, and struggle to make tough decisions. Could their lives really be as glitzy and glamorous as the wine magazines made them out to be? To my surprise, I learned more about myself during this journey than I anticipated. Sharing moments with these successful women inspired me to stop doubting myself. Their examples encouraged me to pursue and press on, no matter what bumps in the road lie ahead, and they gave me hope that if you are passionate and believe in what you are doing, work is not a job but a life.

A Leap of Faith

Just as Leslie Sbrocco (the author of *Wine for Women*) and Michele Ostrove (the founder of *Wine Adventure* magazine) faced a similar quandary, I needed to figure out how to combine my passion with a career that would support me.

I graduated from the University of Delaware in 1988 with an English/journalism degree, but as with so many of us who don't actually do the job they thought they would, I got hooked on the technology instead of on the writing when I landed my first job in a television newsroom. I was intrigued and fascinated with computer technology, and I couldn't get enough of it. That curiosity led me to work in marketing the technology used by broadcasters worldwide. I ended up traveling the world, learning so much, meeting people at every television studio, film studio, and production facility—and wining and dining with them all. It was the best experience of my life, but I encountered something I never expected.

As I moved up the ranks, I became greatly aware of being the only woman in the department, the first woman at a director's level, and often the only woman at executive retreats and events with sixty or more men. I was fortunate that the chairman and the top executives in the company truly believed in my abilities and treated me very well, but with other levels of management and peers I felt that I was treated differently. I had never felt this way while growing up in a house full of sisters and no brothers—a similar experience to that of many women I spoke to in writing this book.

Just like Stephanie Putnam, the winemaker at Far Niente, I was taught by my parents that I could achieve anything. I never considered gender: male versus female. Like Stephanie, I, too, was an athlete and a five-foot-tall woman; I could hold my own when it came to physical ability.

Just like Merry Edwards of Merry Edwards Wines, I encountered rejection in the work world based only on my being a woman. I

knew I was better than most of the men I worked with, so I pressed
on, determined to fight stereotypes by being the best I could be. A
year later, my hard work paid off, and I took over from "one of the
boys."

I stayed in that job for five more years and through two more promotions, but as I moved higher up the ladder, my career became less
fulfilling. I missed being with people and connecting with them
around the world. I missed the creative side of my work. I missed
sharing a bottle of wine over dinner while meeting new friends on
the road. Like Stephanie Putnam, the winemaker at Far Niente
(chapter 18), I second-guessed my abilities and the reason for my
promotion, and I yearned to find my purpose and spread my wings.
I explored other companies but became increasingly unhappy. At
the same time, I sadly got divorced and was forced to find a new
path in both my life and my work.

It wasn't a promotion, a corner office, material things, or power
that would feed my soul and make me happy. I truly felt an inner
yearning to be involved in my community and work with local
charities but, most important, to be with friends and family. I also
needed to be creative and independent. Now that I was divorced, I
was supporting myself without the safety net that another income
can bring, but I knew in my heart that I needed a complete change.
I needed not just a new job or a different company, but to alter my
life. Here I was, sitting in my house, sipping a little wine, and
watching television with my two cats—fretting about a mortgage to
pay on my own and thinking, "What am I doing? It would be easier just to go back to a job in New York City."

It took me only one interview to know that the Women of the
Vine were going to inspire me and give me the courage to write this
book and to find a publisher. My first interview was with Heidi
Peterson Barrett. I was very nervous—this was the woman who
made Screaming Eagle and the only person in the world to get four
perfect 100-point scores from Robert Parker. What a woman to
start off with! I thought, "Who do I think I am, assuming that I can

do this? Maybe this is a bad idea, and nobody will want to read this book." I had all the self-doubts that many of us feel as we face our fears and head into unknown territory.

Heidi quickly made me feel at ease. She opened up to me and shared that she has a life, a family, a home, hobbies, and dreams. Here is a woman who comes into our homes, connects with our families at our dinner tables, and shares her wine with the public to enjoy, but she is real. She is a person. She is a winemaker. She is a woman—like me.

That night I enjoyed sipping some good cabernet sauvignon (unfortunately, not Screaming Eagle), and I mused over my wonderful conversation with Heidi and how she hadn't known what she wanted to do when she went to University of California–Davis and "how she was often the odd woman out" when she started in the wine industry.

At this point, I was hooked and wanted more. I needed to build up my confidence that I was doing the right thing. I also realized that if I became so inspired by these stories, why wouldn't others? As Toni Morrison's words echoed in my head, I knew I had to write the book.

The Women Who Inspired Me

There was no turning back now. I had to believe that others, women and men alike, would enjoy reading this book. As it did me, it would empower others and make them feel good at the same time that they learned about the world of wine.

As I interviewed each woman, I found that it was easy to find the courage to write and to stay motivated. How could I not? How could anyone be afraid to make a change after speaking with Amelia Ceja of Ceja Vineyards and hearing how she overcame incredible obstacles by entering this country at the age of twelve and not speaking a word of English? Why should people doubt whether they can make a career change after speaking to Kimberlee Nicholls, a winemaker at Markham Vineyards, who didn't know anything about wine and was in dental school when she decided that wasn't the career for her? Could anyone really do wrong by going into a new career when Marketta Fourmeaux had the guts to begin a new life in a new country, packing up everything from France and coming to California with just a dream and a prayer? Should anyone feel intimidated by exploring the world of wine when even Kristin Belair, the winemaker at Honig Vineyard and Winery, admits that she is confused by the vast number of choices on a wine list?

When you question whether you are able to inspire others with your work, read about Stephanie Browne, the founder of Divas Uncorked, and her work to start the first wine club for African American women, an audience all but forgotten by the wine industry. Every time you hear that voice of doubt in your mind, sit down, relax, pour some wine, and recall the wonderful stories of these women.

Meet the Women

Par one of the book gives a brief overview of the winemaking process and provides a good background on the responsibilities and the hard work that come with the title of winemaker. Many people are not familiar with the scope of the profession and the entire winemaking process. This chapter will help you to appreciate this tough job as you continue reading the winemakers' stories.

Each chapter in part two starts with an inspiring quote that leads you into the women's personal lives. Each woman's story contains life lessons and knowledge of wine. The women share their lives, their wine tips and pairings, and, most important, their passion for wine.

I invite you to read on and join me in a toast to the Women of the Vine!

Part One

THE WINE

Meet the
Winemakers of
Women of the Vine

1. Heidi Peterson Barrett—La Sirena, Screaming Eagle (ch. 8)
2. Kristin Belair—Honig Vineyard and Winery (ch. 3)
3. Amelia Ceja—Ceja Vineyards (ch. 4)
4. Merry Edwards—Merry Edwards Wines (ch. 10)
5. Marketta Fourmeaux—Château Potelle (ch. 7)
6. Gina Gallo—Gallo Family Vineyards (ch. 6)
7. Stephanie Gallo—Gallo Family Vineyards (ch. 12)
8. Milla Handley—Handley Cellars (ch. 2)
9. Lee Miyamura—Meridian (ch. 16)
10. Paula Moschetti—Frog's Leap (ch. 15)
11. Kimberlee Nicholls—Markham Vineyards (ch. 11)
12. Ramona Nicholson—Nicholson Ranch Vineyards (ch. 13)
13. Stephanie Putnam—Far Niente (ch. 18)
14. Darice Spinelli—Nickel & Nickel (ch. 20)
15. Signe Zoller—Consultant, Zoller Wine Styling and Winemaker (ch. 21)

1

FROM VINE TO WINE

The Job of a Winemaker

ONIGHT, AS YOU SIT AT HOME OR IN A RESTAURANT enjoying a bottle of pinot, stop and think for a moment about what it took to get this wonderful wine to your table. Winemaking is a long and difficult process that is often not fully understood. It is the winemaker who is ultimately responsible for your enjoyment of that glass after a hard day at work. The winemaker oversees the entire process, from growing the grapes to deciding when they should be harvested, figuring out the best way to blend them, and marketing the finished product.

The winemakers in *Women of the Vine* are not just businesswomen; they are also farmers. Successful winemakers make quick decisions to troubleshoot production problems and keep the process running smoothly on a day-to-day basis. Mother Nature can also interrupt the process, creating all sorts of sticky situations and wreaking havoc on the source of all wines: the grapes. The winemakers in this book explain that grapes are "a volatile product. You don't get a second chance and you have only one harvest a year. You can't just order more widgets. This is it." For these women, there isn't such a thing as a typical day at work. Each day, each month, each year, and each harvest are different.

Winemaking also varies according to the winemaker, the winery, the region, and the country. Each different technique and recipe helps the winemaker to create her unique wine style. The responsibilities of a winemaker can change if she oversees a large winery versus a small winery, but either way it is a tough, stressful job and a true labor of love for these amazing women.

A Day in the Life of a Winemaker and the Winemaking Process

Each step of the winemaking process is extremely important because each stage affects the quality of the wine. As if the job didn't have enough pressure!

The Vineyard

The winemaker must first communicate with the viticulturist. This is the person who manages the planting of the vines and the harvesting of the grapes. Vinification is the process of making the wine, and viticulture is the growing of the grapes. The viticulturist keeps a watchful eye on the progress of the grapes as they ripen on the vine and continuously performs lab tests to determine the best time to harvest. Science doesn't tell the whole story, and viticulturists will often rely heavily on their instincts and experiences to help them make this crucial decision.

The grape quality will affect the wine more than any other factor does. It is impossible to turn bad grapes into good wine, but, unfortunately, the opposite can be true. Grapes should be processed quickly after harvesting to avoid spoilage, and they are best handled when cool.

Once again, harvesting is such a pivotal time for decision making because the ripening process affects two of the primary compounds for making wine—sugar and organic acids. When a grape ripens, it accumulates more sugar, and this can happen rapidly. Simultaneously, the organic acids decline during the ripening process and can make the grapes shrivel and dehydrate, affecting the amount of juice and causing the clusters to lose weight. Winemakers may decide to allow the crop to hang on the vine and dehydrate a bit (this is called "hang time") so that more of the flavors can develop and also to help them determine the best time to harvest. Once the winemakers decide to harvest, however, grapes are picked as rapidly as possible and with the least amount of damage to the grapes.

Wineries use two methods of picking—manual or machine harvesting. Manual harvesting can be done quickly if you have a lot of hands on deck. Although it is a more selective and thorough process that minimally damages the grapes, it is not cheap. Machine harvesting can be much less expensive, but winemakers bear the cost in damaged vines and the number of good grapes that survive to be crushed. It can take about a hundred pounds of grapes to make between five and seven gallons of wine. The amount of juice extracted will depend on how juicy the grapes are and how efficient the pressing is. You can usually get approximately five 750-milliliter bottles of wine per gallon of juice. When you think about the scale of wine production in the United States, that requires a lot of grapes! Besides cost issues, a vineyard's topography and layout can largely determine the type of harvesting that a winery chooses. Hilly vineyards are difficult to machine harvest and are almost always harvested by hand.

The Crush

The winemaker now has to oversee the crushing and the pressing of the grapes. First, the destemming process separates the stems from the grapes. Then the grapes are pressed, which removes the juice and leaves only the solids, such as the seeds and the skins. To make white wine, the skins have to be removed immediately to separate them from the juice. It is the skins that affect the color, the flavors, and the tannins if they stay in contact with the juice for too long. Tannins occur naturally in plants, and in wine they come from the grape skins. They are responsible for the degree of a dry, puckery sensation in red wine, and they also help to naturally preserve the wine. When winemakers make red wine, they may choose to leave the juice with the skins and the pulp (sometimes for up to eighteen days) to give the juice more of the pigment, the tannins, and the flavors. The technical term for this process is *maceration.*

Many people think that sulfites are the cause of the ill effects they feel after drinking wine, but, actually, the practice of keeping the juice with the skins is to blame. The term *sulfites* is often used when people talk about wine, and sulfites may be listed on the back label of most wines you enjoy, but all wines contain a small amount of sulfites from the fermentation process. Some winemakers choose to add sulfur dioxide as a preservative, but with today's technology, it is used far less than ever before. Approximately 1 percent of the general population and 5 percent of asthmatics have an allergic reaction to sulfites, according to the Food and Drug Administration. Sulfites can be found in many prepared foods in the supermarket and in convenience stores because food manufacturers also use them as a preservative. So, contrary to popular belief, sulfites don't cause those nasty headaches you get after drinking too much wine, especially if the headaches occur after you drink red wine, because white wine contains even more sulfites than red does.

So how are the grape skins the culprit causing this ill aftereffect? Fermented foods and drinks contain two naturally occurring chemicals: histamines and tyramines. Histamines are in the skins of the grape and are responsible for dilating blood vessels in the brain. Tyramines do the opposite; they constrict your blood vessels. Either one of these chemicals can cause headaches. Red wines generally have a higher concentration of histamines and tyramines than white wines do because red wine spends more time in contact with the skins.

Alcohol and Malolactic Fermentation

There are two types of fermentation: alcohol and malolactic. Alcohol fermentation is a natural process that occurs during the conversion of sugar into alcohol. This usually begins on its own due to natural yeast found in grape skins, or sometimes winemakers will add a special yeast strain to get the process started sooner. For red wines, alcohol fermentation can take from five to ten days. White wine usually takes longer—between twelve and fifteen days—so that more of the aroma remains. Drier wines allow all of the sugar to turn into alcohol.

Malolactic fermentation is an option that a winemaker may use more often for red wine than for white. It can happen naturally during the alcohol fermentation process but is not a guarantee, so a winemaker may choose to induce it afterward. This process converts the malic acid that exists naturally in the grape juice into lactic acid. (As a basis of comparison, malic acid is a tart acid that's found in fruits such as Granny Smith apples. Lactic acid is one component of milk.) Malolactic fermentation can soften the wine's acidity, therefore making it more pleasant to drink. When this process is used in chardonnay production, the wine is often described as tasting buttery.

Blending

Before the aging process begins, the winemaker may combine wines made from different grape varieties, such as cabernet, merlot, and sangiovese, and mix them together in vats. This is how many wineries and winemakers create the desired aromas, flavors, tastes, and overall styles of their wines. Wines made in the United States are usually named after the specific variety (varietal) of grape used to make the wine (cabernet sauvignon, chardonnay, and merlot).

Kimberlee Nicholls (chapter 11) describes this in her story, and it is the simplest explanation. She uses the apple analogy: "You have different types of apples. You have Gravensteins and you have pippins and you have Yellow Delicious—and grapes are the same. They all taste a little bit different." In Europe, it is more common for wines to be named after their appellation (the region) where the vineyard, the winery, or both, are located (Bordeaux, Burgundy, Chianti).

Aging and Racking

Wine can be aged either in barrels or in steel tanks. When aged in oak barrels, the wine will take on an aroma and a flavor that are described as toasty, vanilla, or spicy. A winemaker may instead choose to age the juice in the stainless steel tanks so that it will have a crisper and more natural fruit flavor. This process can take up to two years for red wines but is much shorter for white wines, sometimes only a few months to a year. During the process, the winemaker may move the wine from one container or barrel to another. This is called racking and is basically decanting on a grand scale. This process transfers the clear wine from one barrel to another barrel, leaving behind any sediment that can spoil the wine. The result will make for a much clearer wine. The first racking usually takes place approximately two to three weeks after the fermentation process is complete. At this stage, the heavier particles will already have settled at the base of the container. The best way to implement this procedure is by using a siphon to move the clear juice away from the particles. A winemaker may rack the wine several times (sometimes three or four times) at set intervals until there isn't any more sediment. Now, the winemaker is ready for the next and final step—bottling the wine.

Bottling

Some wineries may choose to filter the wine prior to bottling. This fining or filtration is an additional and final way to remove any sediment from the wine. It can also help to preserve the wine in the bottle. Now the final stage has arrived, but it's often the most stressful. The winemakers have tested, tasted, and blended, and the wine seems perfect and ready to go—bottling will be the last step. The wine is done. This is the last chance to include additives and to make adjustments—to create the best wine possible. If anything needs to be fixed, it can't be done after bottling.

Storing and Serving Wine

What about opened wine? What is the best way to store an opened bottle? Many people have experienced coming home after work and opening a bottle of wine just to relax and enjoy dinner, a TV show, or a chapter in a good book, but they don't want to consume the whole bottle that evening.

Wine is very delicate when it is opened because contact with air and oxygen affects the wine. Oxygen is wine's enemy; it causes fruit to fade and the balance of the wine to change. When stored properly, wine can be enjoyed another day. Remember that heat speeds up oxygenation, so keeping wine in the refrigerator after opening it will slow this process down. Recorked wine can last between two and three days in the refrigerator. Red wine can be stored this way, too, but let it warm up before it is consumed the next day. If you prefer to store opened wine longer, consider buying a stopper and a pump at a wine store or online. The key is for the pump to remove air from the bottle; then the stopper can form an airtight seal to keep any additional air from seeping in. Another option is to buy a gas preservative that comes in a canister. Simply spray the gas into the bottle and quickly replace the cork. This method is considered a bit less effective, so the wine may still spoil. If spoilage occurs, consider this little cooking tip: oxygenated wine is not bad; it will taste and smell funny, but it won't harm you. Use it in cooking your next meal so that you don't have to pour it down the drain.

If you plan to consume a newly purchased bottle within the next six months, think about investing in a wine rack. Horizontal wine racks are best so that the wine stays in contact with the cork; otherwise, the cork can dry out and even shrink over time, causing air to leak in and oxygen to contaminate the wine. Vertical racks are often used to display wine in stores or restaurants where the wine won't sit for very long in that position.

The rack's location in the house is also essential. Wines do best if they are at a stable, cool temperature and free of vibration. Even though the nice little racks that sit on top of the refrigerator look good, they can be exposed to heat, light, and vibration, which can spoil the wine over time.

When serving wine, you may decide to let it "breathe" a little before you drink it. This practice often confuses wine drinkers because oxygen is touted as the enemy. The key is to learn which wines need time to breathe and for how long. You can allow a wine to breathe by either opening the bottle prior to serving it or by putting the wine in a decanter or a carafe. White wines and sparkling wines generally do not benefit from breathing, but some red wines that are very tannic (they have a bitter, dry, puckery effect in your mouth) can benefit a lot from breathing. The oxygen mixing with the tannins can help to soften the effect, making the wine more pleasant to drink. Keep decanting in mind for a young (consumed within six to twelve months after bottling), full-bodied red with a lot of cabernet sauvignon grape or an Italian wine like a Barolo or a Brunello that is up to six years old when first bottled. If you decant, make sure it is no more than about an hour before the wine is served. If it is left to breathe too long, the oxygenation process cannot be stopped and can affect the taste and the smell.

It's Done—This Year's Harvest!

Winemaking is a tough job and one that requires hands-on work, quick decision making, teamwork, knowledge, experience, and a whole lot of self-confidence. It is a long-term cycle each year, and every year yields a new crop and new problems to solve. Despite this, every one of the winemakers in this book loves her job.

Now for the Fun Part—Selecting the Wine!

We have all experienced the daunting task of reading a huge wine list at a restaurant or walking into a wine shop with rows and rows of wine staring at us from every corner of the store. What do we pick? How can we possibly be familiar with all the wine choices out there? It is an intimidating world, and even winemakers feel it. The choices are overwhelming, and once the marketing messages are introduced, it gets even harder to determine our likes and dislikes.

The most important thing is to know what you like. No one tells you whether you like pears or bananas, so why should chardonnay or riesling be any different? Your palate and your preferences are part of what makes exploring wine and food so enjoyable. Just as with food, there are ways to narrow down your choices and get a better idea in advance whether you will find a wine's flavors agreeable. If you don't like spicy food, you may not eat curry, but if you love peppery foods, then a good steak au poivre may be just the dish you crave. With wine, it is the same. How do you learn what you like and what flavors and smells are in each variety of wine? One tool is featured in this book. Dr. Ann Noble truly changed the face of the wine industry when she invented the Wine Aroma Wheel.

The Wine Aroma Wheel

Dr. Ann Noble is known internationally for her work as professor and sensory scientist/flavor chemist at U.C. Davis in Sacramento. Ann set out to describe the aromas of wine by compiling terms that would also allow others to do so. These words needed to be descriptive, not subjective. Ann wanted wine to be experienced by everyone; therefore, everyone should be able to talk about it comfortably, even at home. She compiled a long list of terms for white and red

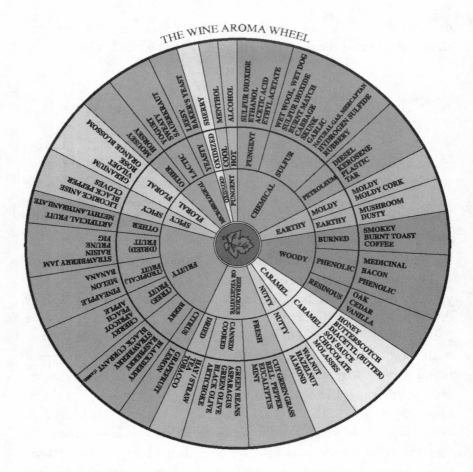

Wine Aroma Wheel. Colored plastic, sparkling wine, and table wine wheels are available for purchase at www.winearomawheel.com.

wines, and she sent the lists out to a broad segment of the wine industry until she narrowed down the terms and organized them in a circle graph. The Wine Aroma Wheel was first published in 1984 and then again in 1987, this time including the recipes for making the standards to learn how to identify the aromas. Ann recently received the Merit Award of the American Society for Enology and Viticulture for her significant accomplishments in the wine industry, and *Decanter* magazine named her one of the ten outstanding women in the California wine industry. She also taught many of our other women winemakers at U.C. Davis.

Using the Wine Aroma Wheel

The general terms are located in the center of the wheel, and the most specific ones are in the outer tier. Ann tells us that "these terms are *not* the only terms that can be used to describe wines, but represent ones that are often encountered. Novice tasters often complain that they 'cannot smell anything' or can't think of a way to describe the aroma of wine. Fortunately, it is very easy to train our noses and brains to connect and quickly link terms with odors." The easiest way is to do an exercise that Ann describes to teach yourself how to differentiate the main aromas in wine. (Also try the exercise that Merry Edwards explains in chapter 10, which is a similar test to train your taste buds.)

All you need to start may already be in your cabinet or refrigerator or is readily available at your grocery store. The one ingredient that Ann knows is not available is linalool, a naturally occurring chemical with many commercial applications such as in perfume and soap, which she uses for the aroma of riesling, gewürztraminer, or muscat wines. She has a handy trick for us to use at home. "For this distinct floral, citrus aroma get handi-wipes. Put [an] opened handi-wipe into an empty covered glass. [A]lternatively, bring some Froot Loops (a breakfast cereal) and put them dry into an empty wine glass. Sounds silly, but either makes a good linalool standard." Following is an excerpt from Ann's guidelines.

WHITE WINES

If you are just beginning, then it is easier to evaluate white wines; start by selecting some wines with large differences in flavor. For example, include an oaky, buttery Chardonnay (most Australian, or California ones will do), for a "vegetative" (bell pepper, asparagus) Sauvignon blanc, wines from Sancerre or a Sauvignon blanc from New Zealand or cool parts of California will suffice. A floral Riesling or Gewürztraminer from cooler parts of California (North or Central Coast), Oregon, Germany, Alsace (France) will provide a further contrast. If you wish to use a fourth wine, you could try an unoaked Chardonnay (IF you can find it), non-vegetative Sauvignon blanc or include another variety such as Viognier.

Make some standards in a neutral white wine (usually an inexpensive jug white wine will work well). . . . [Combining them with the following foods.]

White wine aroma standards
(in 1 oz neutral white wine)

Asparagus   (several drops of brine of canned asparagus)
Bell Pepper   (tiny piece of bell pepper; don't leave in too long)
Vanilla   (Drop of vanilla extract)
Butter   (drop of butter extract)
Clove   (One clove, don't leave in long)
Citrus   (~1 teaspoon of *fresh* orange and grapefruit juice)
Peach   (several teaspoons of peach or apricot puree or juice)
Pineapple   (1 teaspoon juice)
Honey   (1–2 Tablespoons)

From this point on, anything goes; smell the wines first, smell the standards, start to see which terms describe which wine. If you come up with NEW terms such as lichee/lychee—make the standard! Smelling the BASE WINE makes it really easy to identify the spiked aromas by contrast.

RED WINES

For the first red wine tasting, choose wines with very different aromas, such as a pinot noir (Carneros or very cool central coast area of CA, Oregon, or red Burgundy), a Cabernet Sauvignon (for vegetative, get a wine from a cooler CA region), for less vegetative, try Napa, Sonoma, or Washington (CA) a black peppery Zinfandel. The standard "recipes" for most frequently encountered red wine aromas are below. [Use a jug red wine to add the flavors to, as you did with the white wine.]

Red wine aroma standards
(in 1 oz neutral red wine)

Asparagus   (several drops of brine of canned asparagus)

Bell Pepper   (tiny piece of bell pepper; don't leave in too long)

Vanilla   (Drop of vanilla extract)

Butter   (drop of butter extract)

Clove   (One clove, don't leave in long)

Soy sauce   (few drops, great for older reds)

Berry   (Mix of fresh/frozen berries and/or berry jams)

Berry jam   (1–3 tablespoons OLD straw-berry jam) (for older Pinot noirs)

Artificial fruit   (add few crystals of red [Kool-Aid] powder)

Black pepper   (few grains black pepper)

Anise, black licorice   (use few drops of anise extract)

SPARKLING WINES

Sparkling wines need different terms than those on the wine aroma wheel. In addition to citrus and berry standards, here are some of the most relevant ones, especially those with long aging on the yeast lees before being disgorged.

Sparkling wine aroma standards
(In 1 oz of neutral white still wine)

Lime   (A few drops of Rose's [L]ime Juice or squeezed lime juice)
Apple   (Sniff freshly cut apple)
Toasted hazelnuts   (Crushed nuts alone)
Sour cream/yogurt   (1 Tbsp. in empty glass or wine)
Vegemite   (tiny amount of Vegemite)
Cherry/strawberry   (Few drops of flavored juices or extracts)
Nutmeg   (few grains)
Caramel   (crush one Kraft caramel)
Vanilla   (as above for table wines).

[Don't be afraid to add more "stuff" if the aroma is not identifiable; dilute it with the base wine if it is too strong. Put the standards in wine glasses, and cover them with plastic wrap to increase the intensity of the aromas and to prevent the odors from permeating the entire room.]

Defects
[This is another good test to try. Sometimes we question our own sense of smell and can't tell whether something has gone bad. Here is a good way to identify whether the wine is oxygenated or turning bad.]

Some of the commonly encountered wine defects can also be illustrated by making standards.

Moldy Cork   the BEST standard is the actual example of the defect. The cause, TCA, trichloroanisole will leave a lingering odor in your home!
Volatile acidity (VA)   Few drops of Ethyl Acetate or nail polish remover

Acetic acid   A few drops vinegar

Oxidation

Acetaldehyde   few drops of sherry

Sulfur

H_2S Hydrogen sulfide boiled egg or black sand from Japanese food store

Ethyl mercaptan   Smell of natural gas (tell people to experiment on their own carefully)

SO_2 Sulfur dioxide   Dried apricots (which were treated with sulfite)

Brettanomyces (A wild yeast)   Drop of creosote or piece of old fashioned Band-Aid (a horsey, barnyard smell)

Part Two

THE WOMEN

2

MILLA HANDLEY

Winemaker, Handley Cellars

You start out with one thing, end
up with another, and nothing's
like it used to be, not even the future.

—Rita Dove, from the poem "O"

WHEN MILLA HANDLEY WAS A KID, SHE COMPETED with her sister for her father's attention, as many daughters do.

Milla remembers evenings around the dinner table. "We drank wine at dinner every night or a lot of nights. My sister just doesn't get it—she doesn't like wine. She's only eighteen months older than me, but she's still my older sister, and she could do everything better than I could. She had the ability to flirt. She had the ability to use her wiles to get what she wanted. On the other hand, I usually picked the worst moments to say, 'I need this,' when my father was already in a rage about something else. My sister had great timing. She'd say to herself, 'Okay, this is not the right time to ask for something.' I didn't have that ability."

Milla, however, did possess talents of her own to impress her father that her sister didn't share. "There were two things I could do that she couldn't. When I was little, I always liked hot sauce, and my dad was into hot sauce. So I could eat hotter foods than anybody except my father. My mother says that when I was two years old, I got hold of a bottle of Tabasco sauce, took a glug from it, and said, 'Mom, there's pepper in there.'"

Milla's second ability ended up changing her whole life. "I liked wine when I was a little kid. We were always allowed to have a sip, and I liked it and my sister didn't." Thus a winemaker was born out of innocent sibling rivalry.

"When I went to U.C. Davis, I was going to be an art major, but that really didn't work out well. So I sat down, took a practical look at my life, and asked myself what I wanted to do." Milla realized that an important aspect of her career objectives was in figuring out where such a job would lead her. "I knew I wanted to live in the country. From the time I was little and my mom took me to San Francisco, I didn't like it. Now I actually like cities, but I was fifty before that happened!"

It makes sense that Milla would wind up owning her own vineyard in the tiny Anderson Valley area of Mendocino County, a fifteen-mile stretch of verdant, rolling hills about two hours north of

---

Regarding the celebrity involved in winemaking, Milla has a balanced perspective. "Winemakers do the same thing that chefs do, but I think that most winemakers are closer to being farmers than most chefs are to being gardeners. Alice Waters [of Chez Panisse] said, 'Keep seasonal, local, good farming practices, and then we'll make good food.' Winemakers do the same thing. We spend a lot of time in the vineyards, and it's so important."

Milla Handley

San Francisco. "There are less than two thousand acres planted in the Valley," she says. "It's a tiny, tiny region, but it's very finite and it's absolutely gorgeous. It's really special." Her twenty-five-year-old Handley Cellars resembles a bucolic fantasy. Its large white barn, water tower, and stately main house with a wraparound porch look like the ideal spot to sip a glass of wine and contemplate the benefits of country life. Nestled among the vineyards and gigantic pine trees, Handley Cellars produces fifteen thousand to sixteen thousand cases of pinot noir, zinfandel, chardonnay, and gewürztraminer (which *Gourmet* magazine has lauded), as well as a few other white varietals and sparkling wines each year.

"We are certified organic here," Milla says. She has been committed to organic farming for a long time, although she only recently got the official paperwork in order. "Our basic philosophy is that our wines are varietal, regional, and vintage, and they reflect those things."

For Milla, a lot of her style comes from understanding the personalities of her vineyards and adjusting her winemaking style to them. "This is the female side," she says, "or maybe it's the parenting side. Individual children come out of the womb differently, and your goal as a winemaker is the same as your goal as a parent. You want the essence of what you get from the vineyard to come through in the bottle, but you want to "civilize" them so they can function acceptably in society. They can be accepted in society in the proper place.

"Years ago, in winemaking, I used to back off and do nothing. I had a distributor who worked with a lot of Burgundy producers, and he said, 'No, no, no. You need to be there as a winemaker; you just don't need to overwhelm.' That's similar to being a parent. You need to be there; you need to take those deep breaths sometimes, and sometimes you need to intervene. But in the long run, when your child is mature or your wine is mature, it has to have its individuality. That is my goal as a winemaker."

It's an ambitious goal. The cooler weather of the Anderson Valley makes it the ideal spot for temperate (cool) climate grapes, but as intriguing as these varietals are, they can also be persnickety on the

*W*hat are some of Milla's favorite pairings? "I don't cook duck very often, but duck and pinot are just a given; they just go great together. And if my food is sweet-spicy, like Thai shrimp, I like gewürztraminer and riesling. I think that they're just dynamite. If it gets into the wasabi kind of spicy, sauvignon blanc and sushi are incredible. Sauvignon blanc with an avocado is great—it becomes creamy; with wasabi, it becomes very minerally. To me, it's one of the most incredible food pairings. You can't say whether the sauvignon blanc is better or worse with one or the other; they just change it."

vine—pinot noir, most notoriously. "It's really important with pinot noir to treat each vineyard and each tank as an individual, and not to just have a formula. I love pinot because it has a mercurial, feminine side that I don't think of in cabernet. It has intrigue, and I will quote from memory Dr. Amerine, who was coteaching sensory evaluation when I was at Davis: 'A wine has to have a come-hither quality,' which means that when you take a sip and you put the glass down, you want to take another sip because it's revealing itself in layers, so it's very feminine in that quality. But you just have to go with your gut on these things."

Finding Anderson Valley

Milla's road to winemaking was similar to the paths of many other winemakers I interviewed for this book: she had a background in science. Milla knew a little about food science already because her mom's side of the family was in brewing, and Henry Weinhard of Blitz-Weinhard, a regionally renowned brewery in Portland,

Oregon, was her great grandfather. Her interest in science and wine and her family background in the brewing industry made U.C. Davis seem like a logical fit.

"About that time, my sister moved to Healdsburg and married a guy in the wine industry. She also sold real estate and sold my dad a vineyard up there, so that's how we got involved in winemaking. At that point, there were no microbreweries [in the country]; you had to live in a big city, which was something I didn't want to do."

Milla's brother-in-law got her an interview for a temporary crush job with Château St. Jean. "I dropped off resumes at a zillion places and didn't get any callbacks. I probably wouldn't even have been considered if my brother-in-law hadn't recommended me."

That temporary crush job turned into a three-year stint. "I got married in '76 once my job became permanent at St. Jean. Rex and I had been together for five years. So I had a job, and he was getting his teaching credentials at the time."

Not too long afterward, Milla became pregnant. "It was not a job that left room for motherhood because back in '78, there was a whole lot less flexibility about being a parent in the wine business. I quit St. Jean, and we moved up to Anderson Valley toward the end of my pregnancy with my first child because Rex got a job as a ranch manager at Navarro Vineyards. I loved it. I think it's an incredible place to raise children."

Milla took a year off after her first daughter was born, and she worked part time after that—or, in winemaker's time, two harvests passed before she went back to a winery full time again. She was concerned that it might be hard to find work when she was ready to return, but she was fortunate to have good friends in the business. "I was actually in a tasting group with Jed Steele [of Steele Wines] and Paul Dolan, who used to be the head winemaker and then the president of Fetzer, but now he's with Parducci, and Mark Bixler, who is one of the partners in Kistler Winery. Jed invited me because our kids were in a play group together in Anderson Valley. Once, on the way over there, I said that I was looking for a crush job that year because I wanted to get out of the house."

This offhanded comment prompted Jed to offer Milla a job at Edmeades Winery, where he was the head winemaker. Her youngest daughter, Megan, was one year old at the time, and Edmeades was just down the street from her house. It was an offer she couldn't refuse. "I worked at Edmeades for very, very little money—four dollars an hour and a case of wine under the table, but I didn't know the case of wine was under the table for six months!" she says, laughing. "I worked three harvests there. I started out as crush help, and I ended up doing lab work and cellar work, so I got my experience doing cellar work there. In a bigger winery, you would never get that."

In 1982, Milla started making wine in her basement after realizing that she really wanted to start her own winery. "I learned a lot from working for two winemakers who had two totally different perspectives. St. Jean had all the money they wanted, and Edmeades never really had a good budget and didn't have the wherewithal to make it over the hump for various reasons. They were great winemakers, though, with lots of things going for them. It was really good for me to start very small, because it gave me the ability to do everything."

That perspective allowed Milla to launch her ambitious project in the basement of her home. "I ended up getting a small crusher and a small press and some barrels. A friend of mine had a refrigeration company, and he gave me a tiny tank with a refrigeration unit so I could cool it."

After Milla left her job at Edmeades, she started making and selling her own wine, but that wasn't enough. "I'm a little neurotic about working. Thinking that my winery wasn't quite enough, I got a job at a winery in Sonoma County. We were going to do only two hundred cases, so I figured I could do both. I did my harvest at the winery, and my husband helped out. He never forgot me telling him that he ruined some wine because he hadn't checked the Brix on it one day! The wine ended up getting a gold medal [at the Orange County Fair], so it wasn't a big deal. It was a very small amount of wine, but I came home and I flipped about the Brix test." She laughs. "He always said, 'Yeah, ruining wine gets you gold medals.'"

Even under these less-than-ideal winemaking conditions, Milla knew she was on to something. Her business grew tenfold. "We ended up making two thousand cases. I stole my husband's garage, and his motorcycles had to go out. His precious little motorcycles that he'd built a garage for! When I took the garage, they had to be relegated to a carport. But he survived these ordeals."

Witness to Change

Milla's experience with other wineries was relatively brief (in comparison with other winemakers in this book) before she launched her own business. She was aware of her unique position, as a woman and the mother of two daughters, in an industry that was dominated by men.

"My oldest daughter is in law school, and my youngest is a rhetoric major at Berkeley. My youngest actually may come back up here. I don't know if she wants to be a winemaker, but she wants to intern at a winery. As much as my younger daughter sometimes didn't get exposed to gender biases or being treated differently because she is a woman, my older daughter, who is in law school, sees it a lot more. But my youngest now understands. She works part time at Chez Panisse [a restaurant owned by Alice Waters], and it's a very female place. There is a male wine buyer, but Alice has a very clear vision. For my daughter, it's an incredible place to learn, and it's also an incredible place to work because the structure is set up so that it flows without any dominance. She says that for a restaurant, no one raises her voice. You know what's expected of you; if you don't do it, you're not around long."

While Milla watches her girls grow up and face the realities of the working world, it certainly seems a lot different for young women now than it was when she started out. "In some places it has taken years before female salespeople could even call on certain accounts in downtown [San Francisco] areas. Some of the wine shops in the financial districts were male bastions. The neighborhood shops have always been much friendlier because they have always had a much higher percentage of female customers. But when you're working in the financial district—not that there weren't women in the financial district thirty years ago, but the percentage has increased—you still went to certain places and the company had no female employees in a sales meeting. Sometimes I'd be halfway through the meeting before realizing I was in a room with no women."

Interestingly, Milla admits that sometimes the old gender issues in her industry worked in her favor, but not in the way one might expect. Milla was a pretty shy kid (despite her Tabasco antics with her immediate family). Although she has overcome her timid nature, when people came into the wineries where she worked and wanted to meet the winemaker, she didn't admit her position of prominence at the company and didn't demand that her talents and hard work be acknowledged publicly.

"I'm one of the few women who always took it with a sigh of relief to not be recognized. At one point, my older daughter worked for me, and one day I was on a catwalk cleaning a tank. A salesperson walked in the cellar door, looked up at me, and asked, 'Can I talk to the winemaker?' I said, 'He's in the lab.' I had a co-winemaker at that point who was a guy. Megan looked at me, and I said, 'It's just a salesperson!' I didn't care."

Still, Milla marvels at how much things have changed, including the perspective of young women in the industry. "There is this big difference. You're looking at women in their twenties and thirties in the wine business who say, 'I don't want to do anything that identifies me as a woman; I want to be recognized as an individual.' And I say, 'Get over it!' Now the joke is that if you go to a technical seminar, you actually have to wait in line at the women's room, whereas before it was no big deal."

At Handley, Milla's doors are open to everyone, as long as the person is qualified. "You're considered as an individual, but you're also looked at as a representative, and it's important. That doesn't mean I don't hire guys; I had an assistant winemaker who was a guy, and I now currently have a woman [Kristen Barnhisel]. She's great."

When interviewing Kristen and other potential candidates, Milla ran into an odd moment of potential reverse discrimination that took her aback. "The three finalists whom I was deciding among were two women and one guy. I really, really picked the person I thought would be best, but I actually told the guy that I thought he was going to have child-care issues. His wife commuted to Reno because she's in high tech, and he wanted to commute an hour and a half to get here. He said, 'I have a great baby-sitter!' and I said, 'You have a ten-month-old kid. This is not really where you want to go for a winemaking job when you're going somewhere else in life.'"

Of course, Milla knows what it's like to be a parent and a wine-maker at the same time. Organizations like Women for WineSense have sought out Milla as a speaker, and she certainly has a lot to say on the topic. "At Women for WineSense, we talked about not just being women, but being mothers and how it affects you. It really does affect you a lot, but I think women are willing to talk a little bit more about the emotional things.

"Particularly when you're a winemaker, your life is 24/7, and as a mother, your life is 24/7. How you blend them is how you survive; it just is. Being my own boss, I've been able to pick and choose. Can I zip down in the middle of harvest for two hours and watch a volleyball game or not? I don't have anyone else to ask but me. My daughter knows that I might show up or I might not. You make it up, maybe by working two hours later that night, and you don't go if there's a crisis."

The Change in Season

"There is a joke in the Valley that we may not do every day very well, but we do crises really well." Milla says this laughing—not because the small-town joke is funny per se, but because it's true.

She knew that moving to Anderson Valley would be a great place for her children to grow up, but she couldn't have predicted that the small, tight-knit community would also be her own safety net one day.

At the time of this writing, Milla's husband had recently passed away from Lyme disease, which is caused by bacteria transmitted through the bite of a tick. It can attack a body's joints, heart, and nervous system. It's treatable if caught early enough, but if not, it can be debilitating and deadly. Rex struggled with it for several years, and a week before his appointment with one of the best Lyme doctors in the country (an appointment he waited two years for), he died.

To say that Milla misses her husband doesn't come close to expressing what she, or anyone, feels to lose a spouse. Now, she's trying to get back on her feet after having the rug ripped out from under her.

"I'm doing some things that I have to do. I'm going on a trip with my youngest daughter to France soon. To be perfectly honest, the last two years I haven't traveled at all because my husband had asked me not to be gone more than two nights in a row. So I have not traveled. And this is really a funny thing. There are certain things that we resent, and there are certain things that even if we resent them, we really need. Rex was a person who usually said, 'You're overdoing. Don't do this.' Now I have to learn to say no on my own."

Milla has always had an extremely independent spirit, but certain things take getting used to when you're on your own for the first time in your life. The push and pull of important relationships gives an invisible structure to the days, weeks, and years. It's the kind of thing that's not palpable until it's gone.

"About eight years ago, I called my husband on the way back from a very difficult trip. I said, 'Hon, I'm having a midlife crisis,' and he said, 'Oh, God, what's that mean?' I told him I wanted to get a horse again, and he was so relieved. I have a horse, and I used to ride a lot. Sundays are always the day, even in the dead of winter, that I groom my horse, Rocky, and clean his feet. But if it's not raining, I do a little more stuff with him even if I'm not riding him.

"The Sunday after my husband died, I went down there and I just remembered how many times when I came from work and had three extra hours that Rex said, 'Go get on your horse, go get on your horse!' And I hate being told what to do!" Milla laughs. "I always said, 'Why are you nagging me?'"

Her husband's answer was a lot like Milla's own dealings with her pinot noir grapes—they're all individuals, and you must treat them as such. "He said, 'Because you come home happy.' And I remember how much he pushed me into going out. He said, "If you don't have time to ride your horse, then go for a walk—I'll go with you.' Because otherwise, he knew that I would go [back to work]. I just remember how important that was. I haven't been riding Rocky much. We've had way too much rain. But it's drying up, and he has shoes on now. I've ridden him once, I think, since Rex died. Rocky was a sanity check, because otherwise I have a tendency to be neurotic and work seven days a week. So having kids at home and a husband gave me balance." Milla is finding that balance in her own way now—but, rest assured, the blend will be complex and rich and have a very, very long finish.

3

KRISTIN BELAIR

Winemaker, Honig Vineyard and Winery

If you take a passionate interest in a subject, it is hard
not to believe yourself specially equipped for it.

—Ethel Smyth, *Streaks of Life*, 1922

EING A WINEMAKER IS ONE OF THOSE PROFESSIONS THAT
is often envied but rarely understood. It's the kind of job
that sounds chock full of black-tie dinners with famous
chefs and flashing cameras, jet-setting adventures to Europe
for exploratory wine excursions, and days of wine sipping and sam-
pling and debating the value of one wine style over another.

Well, maybe for some winemakers. But for Kristin Belair, the
award-winning winemaker of Napa's Honig Vineyard and Winery,
the day-to-day decidedly unglamorous aspects of her job are far
easier to point to. You're more likely to find her wearing a T-shirt
and jeans than a Dolce & Gabbana gown. As for the jet-setting life,
Kristin says most of her time is spent in and around the vineyard.
"That's one thing that is sort of unique about working here," she
says, "because a lot of winemakers do a lot of travel. Michael Honig

feels very strongly that I need to be here. And I tend to agree with that."

And what about all that time winemakers supposedly spend sipping wine and chatting about the vines? "The only little sort of breath I get is in mid-July."

All of this, though, seems to suit Kristin just fine.

"Even if I won the lottery, I'd probably still do this. People sometimes have the attitude that winemakers are like star chefs or Hollywood celebrities. There's that whole glamour aspect of it. And somehow we just sort of sit around and taste wine all day And it's like, well, no . . . ," Kristin laughs. "It's actually a lot of work."

The path to Honig, or to the wine industry itself, wasn't exactly a direct one for Kristin. She was born in North Tarrytown, New York, but at age one, her family moved to Alberta, Canada, where in all likelihood she would have remained were it not for her parents' divorce. After the split, her mom, a California native, decided to move back home, taking Kristin with her. Despite the upheaval in her young life, Kristin easily took to the outdoor lifestyle of California, but by the end of high school she wasn't sure of her next move.

"I ended up going to U.C. Davis straight out of high school. I was seventeen; I didn't know what the heck I wanted to do! I wanted to be in northern California, not far from home, so I went to Davis. And I did the usual college thing and tried different stuff. I was majoring in biochemistry and just kind of feeling a little lost. I ran into a classmate who had just changed into the enology program."

It's a dilemma many of us can relate to: how do you decide what you want to do with the rest of your life at such a young age? After all, at seventeen most people have barely experienced much outside of the place they grew up. Luckily for Kristin, that chance meeting pointed her in the direction that she would follow for the next twenty-plus years. For the woman who couldn't decide what she wanted to major in during college, let alone decide upon a lifelong career, the siren song of the vineyard became the tune that Kristin found herself humming.

Kristin Belair

$\mathcal{E}$ven though wine is Kristin's big passion in life, she did have one short-lived foray onto another career path: cheesemaking. "I knew someone who was in [the business] and thought, what the heck. It's fermentation, I might as well give it a try!" She laughs. "I only did that for about a year and never got real in depth about it. But I do have an appreciation now for cheese." Lucky for her, it goes awfully well with wine.

"One of my biggest problems is being able to focus on one thing. That's one of my biggest challenges. I've always had a really broad range of interests. And one of the things that's challenging but also really great about the wine industry is that it's such a broad field. There's microbiology, there's agriculture, there's soil science, there's geology, there's PR, marketing, chemistry. And then there's the whole sort of artistic part of it. So I tried it, and I liked it! And I stuck with it."

Right out of U.C. Davis, Kristin landed her first job at Trefethen Vineyards. Although she wouldn't stay for more than a few months, it was an interesting spot for Kristin to begin. While Trefethen is a winery that works with the varietals well known to the West Coast —cabernet sauvignon, cabernet franc, and chardonnay—it also has its line of eccentric rieslings, a grape more famous for its German and Austrian roots and, as of late, award-winning bottles from the Finger Lakes region of New York. Like the sauvignon blanc Kristin creates today at Honig, riesling is not exactly the varietal that comes to mind when most people think about California. Whether it's been intentional or happenstance, Kristin seems to have gravitated toward the road less traveled in the California wine world—and at Trefethen, she was starting at the bottom of the barrel, so to speak!

"Well, it wasn't a permanent job. It was a harvest job. I was basically a cellar rat; cleaned tanks, did pump-overs, learned as much as I could. I was the only woman there, in the cellar."

This, of course, was the norm in the early 1980s, but Kristin was not deterred. "On some level, you could say, yeah, it was a challenge. But I just sort of just ignored it and did the best job I could do."

Still, Kristin did hit a glass ceiling along the way, which she recalls unfettered, revealing a patient nature so key to a winemaker's personality. "I interviewed for a job, and part of the interview was they wanted me to do some tasting. The person in charge basically said, 'Well, you have a really good palate, but I'm not going to hire you— I don't hire women.' Just flat out to my face! And I was like, oh, this is interesting. I guess I don't want to work there anyway!" Kristin didn't miss a beat. "You know, you always have a choice about how you react to something. It wasn't like it was going to make me give

---

*I*f Kristin is one thing, she's certainly down to earth (which, when you make a living with a product of the soil, is a good trait to have). Her utter lack of materialism might even seem intimidating to those of us with a wallet-busting fetish or two, if it weren't for her self-deprecating sense of humor. "I'm really not that into shopping, although my daughter is. So she makes sure that I dress properly! But let me put it this way. One of my friends once gave me a birthday card of the Dalai Lama opening an empty box and saying, 'Oh, nothing. Just what I wanted!'" She laughs. "So I mean, I'm just not that . . . I like nice stuff, but probably the best gifts of my life were my husband and my daughter. I know I'm sounding sort of sappy and sweet, but it's the truth."

---

up. It wasn't like it was going to change what I was going to do. I just wasn't going to do it there."

Simple Pleasures

After that first job at Trefethen, Kristin had an opportunity to head to Australia, where she worked at a few small wineries and absorbed all the wine-making knowledge she could. Back in the States, she took a job in 1985 at Johnson Turnbull Vineyards, where she honed her craft for thirteen years. The wines she made there, especially her cabernets, were lauded by the press, but by 1998, she was ready for a new challenge. Michael and Elaine Honig were looking for a winemaker who could add some personality to their cabernet program but who was still willing to work with a slightly maverick varietal to California, sauvignon blanc. Eight years later, the tiny twenty-five-person operation at Honig still has her full attention.

*B*esides wine, what's one of Kristin's other passions? "I love to cook. I started cooking actually quite young, baking bread by the time I was ten. Sometimes my husband says, 'You don't have to cook tonight.' And there are nights when I don't feel like cooking, but for me it's kind of relaxing." As far as her perfect pairings go, Kristin is a big fan of mixing things up. "I eat very seasonally, so what I eat in the summer is completely different from what I eat in the winter. For pairings, though, grilled fish with a sauvignon blanc is such a natural. And in colder weather, I might make some braised lamb shanks and probably want to have cabernet or maybe pinot."

"Probably one of the things that attracts me to small wineries is the ability to build. And I think that's where a lot of the art is—it's still an art at that level. We're small. I know the names of everybody and how many kids they have and their kids' names, that kind of thing. It's kind of like a family."

Yet even in a small winery, there are big challenges. "Every day is different and is tied in with the whole agricultural cycle. It's really just a dynamic, changing challenge. I think it's important just to keep up with the broad range of knowledge that I need to have, to keep up with all current developments, all the way from grape growing through what people are drinking. What's selling in the marketplace? What's sort of the new trend?"

She also has the added challenge of being a wife and a mother. Yet Kristin keeps it all in perspective. "Well, for example, if you're an accountant, you've got February and March and April where it's nuts, you know? So I just think the whole work/family thing is really a challenge for everybody. I have a twelve-year-old daughter. She's been coming to work with me since she was a baby!"

The one thing that Kristin finds most challenging will shock you, though: wine lists. That's right—even an acclaimed winemaker gets nervous when asked to pick out just the right bottle for her friends and family.

"I get handed the wine list, and I'm usually the one who gets intimidated. It's just there are so many choices. It's nuts! Maybe that's one reason that you have people talk about the *Wine Spectator*, for example, having so much power, because there are so many wines. I think it's intimidating."

She has found a way to muddle through the inevitable selection process with finesse, and there are tips she's happy to share. "One, you don't need to know everything about wine to order wine. And it's perfectly okay to ask questions! In most restaurants, the staff has tasted the wine and should be able to tell you something about a wine. Second, it's helpful if you understand just a little bit about varietals. You know, chardonnay is typically like this, and pinot noir is like this, just to kind of help narrow it down into basic categories.

Or, if you're looking at European wines, to know that Bordeaux is from a Bordeaux varietal, so it's going to be mostly cabernet. If you know that really basic stuff, just to help keep it simple, you'll be able to sort it out."

Her final piece of advice, though, sounds suspiciously akin to the personal creed that may well have tugged her along on the journey from "cellar rat" to renowned and respected winemaker: "Another thing I always try to encourage people to do is experiment. Try things, and if they don't work, they don't work! Nothing's lost; you've learned something." Words to drink and live by.

4

AMELIA CEJA

President and owner, Ceja Vineyards

> Anyone can make wine, really—but not everyone
> can make wine that tells a story.
>
> —Amelia Ceja

*J*ALISCO, WHICH ROUGHLY TRANSLATES FROM SPANISH TO
mean "sandy place," is a state in Mexico known for its abun-
dance of blue agave—the plant from which tequila is made.
So it's a funny twist of fate that one of America's most exciting women winemakers called Jalisco home for the first twelve years
of her life. Then again, maybe it's fitting: although blue agave grows
in an impossibly arid place, it is actually a hearty but beautiful lily.
Kind of like Amelia Ceja.

Her story is the stuff of award-winning scripts: immigrant parents with little to their name and no formal education but enough
conviction, love of family, and heart to power a large city; a chance
childhood encounter picking grapes side by side with a boy who
would become the love of her life; a "dollar and a dream" chutzpah
that led her to a parcel of land she would fight tooth and nail to

keep, and that would eventually make her the first and only Mexican American president of a wine company.

"I was born in Mexico in a very small village called Las Flores. I lived on a farm. It was an incredible experience to be surrounded with a nurturing extended family. I think that ultimately this is one of the reasons I am so successful now as an adult."

Amelia's father traveled to the United States in order to better support his family, toiling on farms as a migrant worker. He picked melons and lettuce in southern and central California, then worked up through the fruit farms of the verdant San Joaquin Valley, and eventually landed in Napa, where there was ample work in the vineyards. In Napa, though, he saw an opportunity for the future, and in 1967, after gathering all the appropriate paperwork, he relocated his entire family—a move that would forever alter the course of Amelia's life.

"I was twelve years old and I left this idyllic village to come to the Napa Valley. It was during September, right in the beginning of the school year in 1967, that I arrived in Rutherford in the seventh grade. It was just great luck for me—in my little village there was school only up to the sixth grade. So this was perfect. I liked school, and even though I came from a very small village, I was pretty much on par, except for the language—I did not speak a word of English."

So there she was, a petite, fine-boned girl starting junior high, thrown into the California dreamin' culture of the late 1960s as an outsider, a kid who couldn't communicate no matter how desperately she wanted to. It's the type of experience that would have most kids feigning illness to stay home from school and hide under the covers. But Amelia was no shrinking violet—she was a blue agave.

"When I arrived in Napa Valley, there was only a handful of [immigrant] families. Most of the men at that time who would come and work in Napa did not bring their families; they would go back to Mexico after harvest. So very few people spoke Spanish.

Amelia Ceja

*W*hat does the Ceja logo—a bell with the Latin inscription *vinum* (wine), *cantus* (song), and *amor* (love)—mean? "In Mexico, church bells ring to reveal the time, announce community celebrations, or call parishioners to church. We have adopted the bell as our trademark, and symbolically ring it now to invite you to become a part of Ceja Vineyards."

"In my school, the administration didn't know where to place me. There were no classes as there are now for the children [who] arrive from other countries. At the time, the schools in Napa County had absolutely no experience with handling immigrants." Amelia was shuttled into a special education class, a seat she didn't occupy for long. "Of course, I was not [special ed], I mean, I did not have a learning disability. They just didn't know where to place me. It worked well for me because the teacher happened to be someone really wonderful and who actually spoke some Spanish."

Before her first year was over, Amelia went from being the kid in special ed who spoke no English to sitting front and center in the most advanced classes for her grade. "I love academics and I love languages, so it was almost through osmosis. One day I could not quite figure out when one sentence ended and one began—you know when you're learning a language. Then boom, the next . . . I remember after Christmas all of a sudden I actually understood. I'm an independent thinker, which I think ultimately really helped me in being who I am today."

But even with her spongelike capacity to soak up knowledge and her quick immersion into American culture, this bright young girl was aware that her circumstances were a little different from her classmates'. "Most of the kids in the school, their parents did not work in the vineyards. Actually, they owned the vineyards. It was difficult on many levels. But I'm very athletic so immediately I got involved in everything to do with the school. And so I think at that age, as a preteenager, I really didn't notice [being treated differently] because I was so involved in learning and, you know, surviving that I didn't really feel it. But I knew that I had a totally different situation. I was very different."

Discoveries in the Vineyard

Amelia found her stride in her new American school. She didn't just survive—she thrived. During this time, she also made two discoveries that were pivotal to the path she would choose in life, and they were both waiting for her in a vineyard.

"My father was a foreman for this company that managed Mondavi's and Charles Krug's winery vineyards. When we arrived here [in the United States], it was during harvest. My father invited me that first weekend that I was here to go and see what it was all about, so I said sure.

"I remember it as clearly as today. They'd just founded the Mondavi winery. It had only been open a year. My father had all of these people who would come from San Francisco to pick grapes. I told him, 'Well, I want to pick, too!' So he gave me a can, because it was by the piece, and showed me how to do it properly. And then Pedro's dad arrived with his wife and the older kids—Armando was eight and Pedro was twelve, the same age as I was."

Pedro, it turned out, was the man she'd marry one day. But before they discovered their love for each other, they each fell head over heels for something else that day—the grapes of the vineyard.

"We were picking, and I remember tasting a cluster of merlot grapes. I was transformed. Table grapes are so boring because there's not those fabulous flavors that you find in the grapes that are used for wines. I remember a perfectly mature cluster of merlot grapes that I tasted. They were so succulent. I immediately recognized that they were different. If you bit into the seeds, there was bitterness and astringency, but if you just gently pressed it in your mouth, it was the most wonderful, flavorful juice, which I'd never tasted in any other grape. That instant was the epiphany. And the same thing happened to Pedro and Armando, who are now my partners."

You Can Go Back Home

Amelia still had one more lightning-rod experience in store for her, which would take her back to the land she'd left as a child. "I graduated from eighth grade, and I received so many awards, and I had done, academically, very well. I still ate the wonderful food that my mother prepared, and we spoke Spanish at the house, but I was pretty much immersed in the whole American culture.

"But then something happened that was really a turning point. My parents invited me to go back to Mexico after eighth grade to go to a boarding school—and I said yes. I think that was perhaps the most important event of my life. I had lived in a very sheltered small village, and here I go into one of the best academic schools in the country, a boarding school in the beautiful colonial city about forty-five minutes away from where my grandparents lived.

"My parents are really forward thinkers. My mother and my father never went to school one day in their life, but they knew that education would give me mobility anywhere. They could barely pay the tuition, because at the time my parents worked in the vineyards, it was very high. Yet they still felt compelled that I should have that opportunity to go back and explore my own culture. They understood that for me to have a sense of my own heritage, I really needed to go back to Mexico and explore it. And I think that is incredible. Very few people whom I've ever met have really given their children such an opportunity to learn about themselves. It gave me such a sense of who I am and who my people [are] and how proud we are to have such a wonderful history and legacy."

In the end, her parents gave her more than their culture; they gave her the kind of gift that every young woman should be so lucky to have: confidence. "After that, I knew that I could do anything. I felt so secure being in my own skin."

It was the key to her entire future.

Taking a Chance

When Amelia came back to California, her drive was unstoppable. She graduated from high school with honors at the tender age of seventeen and headed to college in Southern California to study nutrition, while Pedro remained up north studying to become an engineer for the biotech industry. Yet despite the miles between them, their interest in each other—and in wine—continued to grow.

"I always thought Pedro was very cute. He's tall, dark, and handsome, but, you know, I was living somewhere else. Throughout our vacations, we would still see each other, though, because there were not a lot of Hispanics in Napa County. You tend to gravitate toward each other. And we were friends, and it was only when we were in college that our relationship changed."

Her summers were spent getting to know Pedro and delving deeper into the world of wine. "I'd always work in the vineyard because I wanted to, although I could work anywhere as a college student during the summer. But I elected to continue working in the vineyards alongside my parents because I really wanted to learn everything about viticulture." Meanwhile, during the school year, Amelia took a job at an up-and-coming restaurant in La Jolla and became obsessed with cooking and wine and food pairing. Still, although she'd been thoroughly bitten by the wine bug, Amelia chose to take a job as a nutritionist after graduation. But fate determined that this was not meant to last long.

"As soon as Pedro and I were married in 1980, we immediately remembered that dream we had when we arrived, and perhaps it was the time to really achieve it. We immediately said, 'Oh, of course, we have to move back to Napa,' because that desire to have a vineyard, it was reborn again."

In the same way that she dove into American culture and academics as a twelve-year-old immigrant new to California, she took to making her and Pedro's dream come true. "It was so funny because we had no money, we had two kids—our oldest, who was just a year, and then we had a newborn—but we started looking for land." As luck would have it, Pedro's mom saw a For Sale sign on a piece of property in Carneros while she was driving home from work one day. Although today Carneros has become known for outstanding wines, especially its pinot noir, at the time almost nothing was there. "In the early eighties, there were only very few vineyards in Carneros, but that was pretty much it. We were one of the pioneers there."

Amelia contacted the realtor immediately, and the very next weekend they went to see the property. "It was at the height of inflation. It cost nearly half a million dollars. But we decided, okay, if we sell everything, we can put all of our financial resources together and we can buy this piece of property."

Although there was a small house on the land, Pedro and Amelia stayed in Silicon Valley so they could keep working to support their dream. "Of course, we had absolutely nothing left to develop the vineyard. A long time ago it had been a plum orchard. There were pears there as well. But when we purchased it, it was pasture for cows."

After about a year, the struggle to hold onto their old dream began to overwhelm Amelia and Pedro. They reluctantly put the land up for sale. "Interest rates were in the twenties back then. We couldn't support it. So, we put the land up for sale—and it was lucky for us no one bought it. We just said, 'Okay, we have to do it.' It forced us to move into Napa. There was only one house on this piece of land that we co-owned with my parents-in-law, and it had a little studio adjacent to it, so that's where we moved in [to the studio]. That was in 1985, and by that time Pedro and I had a third child."

As Amelia is quick to point out, starting a vineyard isn't just about buying the land. If anything, that's the easy part. "It requires a lot of money to develop a vineyard. Depending on the rootstock and all of that, each vine now costs from three to ten dollars. And when you need about thirty thousand or so—well, do the math. You need a lot of money! And that's only just for the vines. That does not include the actual preparation of the soil, the irrigation system, the stakes, the trellises—everything. And then you have nothing because it doesn't produce the year it's planted. But if we had known all of that, we probably wouldn't have gotten into it. So we're glad that we didn't know!"

Thanks to her brother-in-law Armando, who by that time had graduated from U.C. Davis's Department of Viticulture and Enology, they got their first big break: a deal to develop the vineyard by selling grapes to Domaine Chandon for its sparkling wine. They planted the vineyard in the spring of 1986.

"We had our first harvest in 1988. Of course, it was very small, but it symbolized the journey, which was started a long time ago by our parents, you know, coming to Napa. To actually taste it! That was like giving birth to a fourth child."

Today, Ceja Vineyards produces seven thousand cases of wine each year. The business is a family affair, with Pedro and Armando rounding out the roster of Amelia's partners in wine. But Amelia is truly the gas in the engine. She is the president and the chief marketer, she travels the country to meet personally with the distributors, she writes the poetic wording for their labels, and she has learned everything, by hook or by crook, about the wine business, taking classes on everything from viticulture to sales. And then, there were all those years that she, Pedro, and Armando spent picking in the vineyards.

---

*A*melia's thoughts on selecting a wine: "If you like it, drink it; if you don't, don't. Wine should be a part of daily life. A celebration of life and food doesn't only nurture your body; it also nurtures your soul."

"That's the strength that we have at Ceja Vineyards. I mean, your wine can be of the highest quality and delicious, but if the wine does not have a voice to take it to people, only the most immediate friends will know that the wine is great. And I think that's where we are leading the wine industry because each of our wines that we produce, you can close your eyes and you can even feel the way the wind flows through the vineyard."

That voice seems to come from Amelia's past. Her experiences in being from a strong, close-knit immigrant family; of having to work very hard to get where she is; of never allowing herself to be excluded from anything. All of that? It's in the wine, too. "We are literally embracing everyone to join us in a truly magical experience of wine and food, where before it was only the people with perhaps more financial means who had already been introduced to wine. The wine industry was only interested in that group. Well, that is such BS! Because wine, in any other culture where it's prevalent and part of their daily life, people do not dissect it and have to do a major study on it to enjoy it."

Amelia has an open-arms policy for fans of her wine, one that makes you want to ask her whether it's an accident that her ideas sound a little bit like the tenets of the American dream. Amelia quickly has the answer: "Well, we *are* the American dream!"

5

ANDREA IMMER ROBINSON

Master sommelier

When I am trusting and being myself as fully as
possible, everything in my life reflects this by
falling into place easily, often miraculously.

—Shakti Gawain, *Living in the Light*

O N THE COVER OF ANDREA IMMER ROBINSON'S FIRST
book, *Great Wine Made Simple: Straight Talk from a
Master Sommelier*, Andrea stands confidently with perfect
posture, in a power-red jacket holding six glasses of
wine—three in each hand—as if they had sprouted there, a gift
from Dionysus himself. Her hair is short, soft but conservative. She
wears demure pearl earrings and an assured, open smile. The background is red, too. It is eye-catching, and yet there is no mistaking
the overall authoritative look. Its caption might read, "This woman
knows what she's talking about."

And she does. Known to millions for her easygoing but always
informative shows on the Fine Living Channel (*Simply Wine* and
Pairings with Andrea), her numerous wine columns, and her books

(she has four now, plus a wine course on DVD), Andrea is easily America's premier go-to sommelier.

Even so, there may have been a different reason for the bold cover design of her first book. In 2000, when *Great Wine Made Simple* hit the shelves, Andrea had already logged several years as a sommelier for the prestigious wine program at Windows on the World—and was one of only nine women master sommeliers on the entire planet (as of the writing of this book, the number has gone up to fourteen).

"I think one of the most common reactions that I used to get when I would approach a table at Windows on the World to help somebody with the wine list was that they would look a little bit taken by surprise. And I think it was that I was a female. I'd say, 'Yeah, I'm the sommelier. How can I help? What do you have in mind?' And they would say something along the lines of 'Oh, really? Well, okay, I expected you to be . . . taller!' But what they probably really meant was, you know, a man. So that always was pretty funny to me."

The thing about the smile she wears on the cover of her first book is that it's authentic. There's nothing that Andrea would rather do than talk to you about wine. Looking at her, you don't doubt for a

---

*W*hat's a master sommelier? A person who has been awarded the highest professional distinction that exists in wine and beverage service by the Court of Master Sommeliers. A master sommelier not only must be conversant with every international wine known to humankind, but also must be adept in spirits, beers, cigars, and other aspects of dining room service. Andrea was the first woman ever given the distinction of Best Sommelier in the United States by the Sommelier Society of America.

Andrea Immer Robinson

second that this person will teach you something fantastic, and it will be fun. Her easygoing, confident style has allowed her not to get pegged as "a woman sommelier" or even as "the woman sommelier a man can trust!" She's just Andrea Robinson—a phenomenal wine expert with a very palatable message: wine is for everyone, every day.

From Finance to Fine Wine

Raised in Texas and Indiana, Andrea didn't start out to make a career in wine—or food, for that matter. She went the more practical route: finance. But her passion for the sensual things in life was always there. "I was into food before I was into wine. I was an avid cook from the time I was a very small girl. And throughout high school, while my girlfriends were doing whatever high school girls do, I was constantly cooking things."

Andrea headed off to Southern Methodist University in Dallas for a degree in finance and economics. "When I graduated, I was hired to work at Morgan Stanley on Wall Street," she says. "I went there straight out of school and worked there for almost two years. I was already quite interested in wine while in college, but I went ahead and pursued a career that was in keeping with my study track." On the side, though, Andrea continued to learn about wine as well, working as a volunteer on weekends and on some evenings after school as a pourer at a wine school. The more she learned, the more she wanted to know.

"I didn't start out pursuing a career in it. I started out like a lot of people in a different career who pursue it as an avocation. And the more I got into it, the more I desired to see if I could make a living at it. And then, ultimately, I just decided to try it. Pretty much everyone in the particular area of investment banking that I was working in at that time reaches a crossroads when they hit the two-year point. The decision is either that they're going to go to business school and then come back to investment banking, or they're going to go in a different career direction." Andrea chose the latter.

"So that's what I did. I was into it quite a bit before I got to Wall Street and kept pursuing it and then kind of got to a natural breaking point in the investment banking career. The choice was to take the MBA school option or do something different. I kind of did the whole total immersion. I went cold turkey and left Wall Street and took a job doing public relations for a Spanish wine company. So I jumped in with both feet."

Soon afterward, she landed at New York's prestigious Windows on the World at the World Trade Center, an experience that she says was one of the most pivotal in her career. By 1992, she was named its first woman cellarmaster, and only a few years later she'd risen to the top as beverage director, in charge of Windows' much-lauded wine program. Then came the distinction of master sommelier from the London-based Court of Master Sommeliers.

"I devoted a tremendous amount of time not only to learning the product, but to perfecting the craft of service. Most people who follow that track will work in the industry, either in the hospitality setting or in a restaurant or that type of thing. I took the test in the States, and I passed the exam in 1996. I was just twenty-nine years old."

Yet even though she is one of only fourteen female master sommeliers in the world (out of a total of just over a hundred), there are many women sommeliers. Despite the befuddled faces of a few customers at Windows who expected their sommelier to be a man, Andrea has never felt that her gender was an issue in the wine world.

"I think everyone goes through the 'being young in their industry' kind of thing, if they're ambitious at all and they want to be taken seriously, it is sometimes not so easy when you're young. So I don't think that part was particularly any different from any other field," says Andrea, who was only in her early twenties when she began to pursue wine as a serious career. "There are certain contexts or avenues or venues where you're still in the minority, but it doesn't seem to pose a real problem.

"I think in 1976 when Kevin Zraly started the Windows on the World wine school, he talked about how it was 80 percent men or

*I*f you've ever visited Andrea's Web site (www
.andreaimmer.com), you may have noticed that
her logo is a butterfly. "I love the outdoors, and to
me, if there's butterflies and bees around, you know
the land is healthy. So I like the idea of symbols that
are indicators that the earth is healthy."

something like that, or maybe even more. But by the time I was
working with him there, starting in 1990—so, that's sixteen years
ago—it was fifty-fifty. I think that women have been eager students
of wine for a long time."

For Andrea, wine is an equal opportunity employer. Her broad,
unbiased approach certainly has won both male and female fans
over the years. She brings this attitude to people she hires, as well as
to her viewers and readers. "I guess I have tended to work a lot with
women and hire a lot of them, too. But I don't explicitly target one
gender over another. I try to open the door and the world up to
everybody possible."

When you hear Andrea talk about wine, you know she means it.

Popping the Cork

The idea of making things simple is one that Andrea really takes
seriously. Whether it's wine basics, pairing ideas, or even recipes
with a vino twist, she gets a kick out of taking any perceived snobbery out of wine. "I'm certainly not the only one, but there are
plenty of professionals who thought to simplify things and to let
people off the hook for not being experts in wine. And let them
know that they can still have fun without being an expert. You
know, you don't have to be an expert at baseball to enjoy going to a
baseball game."

This is one of her gifts—she puts things in a way that can make even the biggest beer enthusiast want to dabble in the vineyard a little bit. "I think the big thing has also been that professionals have begun to validate wines at affordable prices, where for generations, probably, people had the very clear message from the [wine] industry that if it was cheap, it didn't matter how much you liked it; you had no class and it was bad! And now everyone realizes that's a load of goods, as much as saying that food has to be expensive to be good. Well, no, it doesn't. Eggs and bacon at a diner are great, too."

Price point is a big issue for Andrea. She doesn't push bottles of Château Margaux priced to drain your 401(k). She is more concerned that you find something you are comfortable buying and, even more so, enjoy at the table. "Now, when you know that it's safe, that the wine police won't come and arrest you for spending between six and ten dollars on a bottle of wine, you feel a whole lot better about it. It's a gamble that you can stomach."

The theory works out for the restaurateur, too. "I'd rather have a bottle on every other table [in a restaurant] at thirty dollars than a bottle on every tenth table at seventy dollars 'cause I'm going to make more money and—as important or more important—I'm

---

*W*hat's the biggest misconception that people have about Andrea's job? "They think that you eat and drink lavishly all the time." She laughs. "You do some of that, but first of all, no one's body could handle it if that was what you did all the time! And second, if you're doing it right, you're running around on your feet constantly. You're taking care of customers and you're trying to make sure that the company you work for is happy—you're trying to make sure not only that the wine program is exciting but that it's profitable."

---

going to have happier customers because they're going to have a good time. They're going to get treated to some extra service because getting served a bottle of wine is a little bit of extra attention. And then the food's going to taste better because it's going to be served with a great beverage rather than with a glass of iced tea or something. And what business are we in? We're in the business of *service*. You don't want your customer to think, 'Crap, I just spent all this money, and they made me feel like a jerk!' You know, how stupid is that?"

Even more so than in a restaurant, wine shops can be intimidating to some fledgling wine buyers, but they really shouldn't be. As Andrea says, a wine shop is one of your best sources of information. "Develop a relationship with a good local retailer, and don't be afraid to go in and say, 'I want to spend between seven and ten dollars. Give me your best bet.' And every time you go in, let that be the program. Then you can let them choose for you. They're going to be thrilled to have the opportunity to, hopefully, first of all show their skill at selecting less expensive wines and also to cultivate a regular customer."

For Andrea, breaking down barriers doesn't just stop at the price

---

*W*hat's Andrea's favorite item in her kitchen? "Our cast-iron skillets. My husband John's sister got [his] at a garage sale as a present, because obviously the older and more used, the better! And my husband is such a great cook that I'd rather have his food any day than eat out. My cast-iron skillets are from my grandmother. But as a family, our favorite kitchen item is probably the popcorn popper because we make popcorn almost every day. It is one of the great pairings with wine—barrel-fermented chardonnay and popcorn is one of the great matches."

---

tag. You could say that her ability to make wine terms, tastes, and smells easy to understand is her hallmark.

"It's really hard for people to get their heads around the idea that a wine smells like apples when it's made from grapes. But you have a glass of wine and somebody says, 'This is the fragrance of Golden Delicious apples.' Then you can get your head around that. 'It does taste like Golden Delicious!' You know what I mean?" And if you don't, she'll be happy to explain it to you.

"The reason that those flavors come into the wine is that they're a by-product of fermentation. When you start out with the unfermented grape juice, it's just the smell of grape juice. But once the product ferments, fermentation creates all kinds of trace components in the wine that mimic the scents and flavors of other fruits and other things, including spice or whatever.

"A way to get your head around it is to think about what happens to milk once you ferment and age it. You can smell milk and it smells milky, but then you can smell cheese, and it can smell anywhere from tangy to buttery and nutty to sweat and feet. It's all about fermentation because it really actually creates these trace components. When [scientists] do a chemical analysis of the wine, they find components in there that are in fact the fragrances or flavors coming from other things! They'll find ester, for example, and that gives you the butter flavor or the vanilla you smell."

It's the same for taste as well as aroma. "Saying something is buttery without a glass of wine in your hand to illustrate what buttery is like is really difficult. That's why in *Great Wine Made Simple* I had each chapter present tasting lessons that you could do yourself at home. I told you what wines to buy and how to set up a tasting so that you could learn what grassy or spicy or buttery is."

As far as what she likes to drink, this master sommelier is happy to share that information, too. "Pinot noir is my favorite grape for reds, riesling for whites, and champagne for its style of wine—it's got extraordinary acidity." For pairings, one of her very favorites is sauvignon blanc with goat cheese. "Goat cheese is something that's so easy to find. Even in the supermarket you can get good-quality goat cheese. It's the kind of thing that I would keep around all the time, so that when you have friends over, you'll kind of knock their socks off! Another one is pesto and cabernet sauvignon. That's a really great pairing because it's a surprise for people to realize that certain things go really well together."

Full Glass

You'd think that life for Andrea couldn't get much busier, what with filming two shows, writing books, consulting for such mammoth hospitality companies as Marriott and Hilton, being the first appointed dean of wine studies at the French Culinary Institute in New York, and doing a million other projects to boot. But somewhere in the middle of all this, she's managed to get remarried ("It's been a difficult transition for everyone but me," she says of changing her name from Immer to Robinson) and have a family. Juggling her home life and her career—now, that isn't always easy.

"I think it surely must be like every other career, and the challenge is simply balancing the time demands on both sides. I choose to travel less, for sure, and especially with my daughter, Jesse, having just turned one, that's something that's really important to us. I also have a son who's twelve. You have to prioritize your kids because the amount of time that you have with them is so short.

"When it comes to the career side of things, it really takes a major commitment from your whole family. My husband [John Robinson] is a big supporter of both the career and not missing the kids' childhoods. But I think it's hard for a woman sometimes because she develops a lot of feelings about her identity in the context of her job. For a lot of people in general, both motherhood and professionalism are a big part of your identity. And when they're in conflict, it's like, 'Who am I?'"

Andrea is well aware of the benefits, though—and they go way beyond tasting great wine for a living. "Every day's different. I mean, when I'm shooting, it's a totally different thing from when

I'm consulting with clients or just staying home. When you do this sort of thing, the beauty of being 'freelance' is that you can schedule your own stuff. I'm doing what I love. You know, it has its moments, but I'm privileged to be able to work with something that I love so much."

Nowadays, no one needs to be convinced that the tiny woman with the honey-colored hair and the warm smile is indeed one of the best sommeliers around. In fact, the cover of her second book may well say it all. The background is sunflower-yellow, and Andrea wears a butter-colored, long-sleeved T-shirt. Her hair is longer than it was on her first cover, and she's sitting comfortably with a bowl of her beloved popcorn and a glass of chardonnay, among a couple of other favorites. In her hand isn't a cluster of wine glasses but a mushroom on a fork, whimsically held in the air over her left shoulder like a funny, upside-down exclamation point. There is *one* thing that remains the same, though—her smile.

6

GINA GALLO
Winemaker, Gallo Family Vineyards

Courage is the most important of all virtues, because without
courage you can't practice any other virtue consistently.
You can practice any other virtue erratically, but not
consistently without courage.

—Maya Angelou

ALTHOUGH GINA GALLO GREW UP ON ACRES UPON
acres of Modesto, California, farmland, the longest
walk she ever had to take in her life may have been the
hundred-yard jaunt down the lane to her grandfather
Julio's house on the day she decided to become a winemaker.

"I was thinking, Oh, my God!" she recalls. "I was scared to death."

How can you blame her? Along with his older brother, Ernest,
Julio Gallo grew the family business they'd started in 1933 into a
$1.4 billion success story, with five thousand employees, and with
wine sold in ninety countries, making it one the largest wine producers in the world today. For Gina to march her slim, five-foot,
ten-inch frame into her grandfather's home meant more than
simply asking for a job—she was taking on the responsibility of a
third-generation empire.

She couldn't help herself, though; the allure of the vine was too strong to resist. "I didn't really know I would be a winemaker," Gina says, even though this would seem like an obvious choice for someone from her family. But it's true—in college, she'd majored in business and psychology, two avenues that certainly could be helpful in the wine business but weren't exactly direct paths to the vineyards themselves.

"I questioned it a lot. 'Okay, what does Gina like to do?'" she says, laughing at her attempt to swat away fate. "You never know when you're a kid. I loved sports. I loved being outdoors. When the gardener went on vacation, I loved to mow the lawn, do the watering. I remember when my dad was out in the backyard pruning trees, I loved to follow him around. But you know, as a girl, you are thinking, 'Okay, what's my avenue?' So I really didn't find what I loved to do until after college."

It was during this time that she took a job in wine sales, living at home and dividing her work hours between Modesto and San Francisco. Gina started to see that even to sell the stuff, she needed a more intimate knowledge of the how's and why's of winemaking.

"I thought this would be a good foundation for me to become even better at sales. I asked my district manager if I could take some courses and I went to U.C. Davis [Department of Viticulture and Enology]. That's when I realized, I want to learn more of the wine side. Then it started clicking."

After spending a few months under the tutelage of female enology giants like Ann Noble and Linda Bisson at U.C. Davis, Gina knew she needed to have a talk with her dad, Robert J. Gallo, Julio's son. The Gallo family wine gene kicked in, and Gina couldn't get enough of the grapey stuff. She knew she needed to be a winemaker.

"At the time, the winemakers were all men, but I knew I felt strongly about it. I went home to talk to my dad. I said, 'You know, I am really liking this. I think it is interesting. I want to pursue this.' Right at the beginning, he was very embracing, which was great. But he made a comment. He said, 'Well, if you really feel strongly about it, go down the lane because Grandpa is the winemaker. He

Gina Gallo

What's better than a great glass of wine? A perfect pairing recommendation from a great
winemaker like Gina: "Our family pinot noir—the
Gallo Family Vineyards Sonoma Reserve pinot noir. I
love it. It's hard to find the right one that has character distinct enough. During the fall time up in
Sonoma, we have portobello mushrooms—the Italian
mushrooms—so you go mushroom hunting. My
grandfather started it. I've gone mushroom hunting
with my brother, Matt, and Marcello [Monticelli].
It's a fun thing to do. My pairing would be pinot noir
because, obviously, pinot and mushrooms are perfect
together. But the cool thing about those mushrooms
is that they are very meaty. You can even put cheese
on them!"

is the one. Let him know what you are thinking and see what
thoughts he has on the whole idea."

It was, in effect, like going to Oz to ask the Wizard for courage.

"I headed down there, and I remember sitting down. He was in
what we called the garden room. He was sitting there, and I said,
'Grandpa, I was wondering if there was any opportunity down at
the winery that I could possibly work for . . . kind of explore more
of this.'

"I know that with women moving into these realms, it is not
always easy. But my grandpa embraced it in a positive way. I think
he put me in an area that I didn't realize was going to challenge me.
Probably in the back of his mind he said, 'Oh, she won't last. She
will eventually get married. She will eventually have babies—do
what women should do.' But he would never say that, thank God.
He said, 'Yeah, you know what . . . ?'"

And that was the turning point, the moment when twenty-two-year-old Gina went from helping out with the family business as a salesperson after college to grabbing the reins. When you grow up Gallo, though, it's a little hard not to let the legacy get under your skin.

"There were eight in our family: four boys and four girls. It really was growing up in an agricultural [family]—in the country, on a farm, all the produce right around you. We had horses—we would each get on a horse and go until the sun went down. We lived on a vineyard. We had walnut trees. Every summer, I remember that we would go out and pick the walnuts, and then we would go down to the local feed store and sell the bag of walnuts to them. Stuff like that."

But still, one wonders, didn't that last name loom large? Like Kennedy? Or, more fittingly, Mondavi?

"Not at all. No, no, not at all," Gina says, seeming to marvel at how funny that idea is. "I mean, obviously, I knew it was a family business. It was about the family. I knew we were about wine, but in our family it was about bringing it back to the table. And around our dinner table—because that was one thing, you always had to be at dinner, no matter what—it was great because both grandparents, my mom's and my father's, were over on Sunday, and we would have dinner with them.

"But when I heard what they talked about, what they were doing for the next generation, how they were building things long-term—that really resonated with me, and I felt it."

Loss and Gain

For many of us in the United States, it's not uncommon for our families to be scattered to the four corners of the earth, so it might be a little hard to imagine the close-knit family environment that Gina grew up in: seven brothers and sisters, seventeen cousins, aunts, uncles, and both sets of grandparents gathered around all the time. "If you weren't with your parents, you were with your grand-parents," she says of days growing up on the family farm. "My parents were wonderful storytellers, but there is something about a grandparent. You hear through them about your parents; you hear through them about their great-grandparents, and it really sinks in—at least, for me it really did."

Gina's grandfather died in 1993, the victim of a jeep accident on a ranch road. When Gina lost her grandfather, she didn't just lose the invaluable patriarch of the family, she lost her mentor, too. "To be able to work with my grandfather was amazing," she says of those first few years of learning from Grandpa Julio. His death affected her deeply.

"It was really hard. And that is why I look back and thank God I had been in that arena working with him. You know, it is one thing to have the experience of your grandparents, but then when you work with your grandparents who started the family winery, and see how he was, how he just . . . ," Gina takes a deep breath and composes her thoughts. Behind her bright blue eyes, you can see her searching for the words to describe her grandfather's legacy—but how? In the end, she decides upon an anecdote: "He was demanding and challenging—he would get in a heated debate with Marcello [Monticelli, Julio's handpicked protégé, who became Gina's mentor and is now the master winemaker at the family winery in Sonoma], but then at the end of the tasting, he'd say, 'Well, come over to my house. Let's have a plate of pasta.' Work was work, but when you went home, you were together. You know, that's the balance of life."

A Woman and Her Future

The period after Julio died was hard on members of the family, but their strong sense of connection to one another helped them to band together and muddle through. In some ways, they even found a way to make the family business even stronger.

*O*ne thing Gina is very committed to as a winemaker is practicing sustainable agriculture in the
family vineyards—which basically means farming
practices that will not do any residual damage to the
surrounding environment or the livestock and will
help to preserve the appropriate natural balance of the
land. "My grandfather brought it back to the simplest
things, which I think is really important. He always
said, the quality of the vineyard can be seen in the
footprints of the owner in those vineyards—it is by
being in there and knowing the vineyards. He always
passed on to us that your richest gifts come from the
land.

Now my brother Matt is taking it to a new level,
not only with the environment but in strengthening
the communities where we live and work. So how
does it come together? Managing the soil, giving back
to the land—it is going to give back to you twofold.
So it is a natural thing for me to work in the vineyard
with Matt to try and balance the vine's natural habi-
tat. And today, we are coming back to it more—we
are coming back to the table, we are coming back to
enjoying life, slowing down a little bit." How else
does Gina get back to nature? Like any other self-
respecting California girl. "I love surfing!" she says.

"It was very inspiring to see my dad in those days. He kept a clear
mind and provided a new style of leadership for this transition, a
passing on of the generations. He kept us moving forward, and it
was a natural thing for him. He worked so closely with Julio. They
worked together for so many years, and in many ways he was his
silent partner.

"And he did a tremendous job and that just inspired me even more to think, You know what? There is not just one style. There is a place for everybody. I was still very young, I was still in Modesto. But every day that passed, every year that passed, I still enjoyed really understanding more about wine, reading about wine, working with different people. The key is to have a human element, no matter what business you are in. I don't care how hard, how tough, how driven you can be, the human element has to be there, because if people don't feel that human side, that connection . . . I mean, life is too short, they are going to go elsewhere."

This is the thing that you start to notice about Gina Gallo once you spend a little time with her. She has such great strength, but it all goes back to the things she was taught as a young girl on the farm. For her, taking the lead with her brother Matt in the family business isn't about power; it's about commitment. To her, the family and the business go hand in hand. "It's a family. Once you get bigger, it does get tougher. It is much more difficult, but it's important to keep that human style there."

Now, at age thirty-nine (she laughs off turning forty next year: "I love it. What's the new thing for women? Fifty is the new thirty, or something like that?"), with more than a decade of winemaking under her belt, Gina is a woman in control not just of her own career, but of guiding the good family name in the modern wine industry.

"When you look at it, planting a vineyard is one thing, but for a winemaker, you focus on bringing in those grapes. A lot of the planning happens during harvest—that wine is still evolving throughout the year, but you are working on that same wine. I don't see doing it until I'm eighty, but that is only forty more times. So forty more vintages. That even gets it closer to home. Only forty more times you are going to really create a vintage. That is nothing—nothing."

So, what's next for Gina? With Gallo producing and investing in more small-label versions of its wines and gaining more respect in the wine-drinking world, it seems like a lot of pressure for her to shoulder. Her trademark energy ("I naturally have a lot of energy;

I will probably come out of my skin if I have too much caffeine!")
and love of her job, though, keep her going stronger than any
Robert Parker review could.

"Now we are looking at things and going, 'Okay, so what is next?
Where are we headed?' The reality is, you never just sit. It's always
about continuous improvement. So now, it's up to us, on our shoul-
ders, the responsibility of where we will be headed. For myself, I
create wine, and I absolutely love it, but the thing I love best is that
at the end of the day you put that bottle on the table with family
and friends."

Like grandfather, like granddaughter.

7

MARKETTA FOURMEAUX

Winemaker, Château Potelle Winery

We could never learn to be brave and patient
if there were only joy in the world.

—Helen Keller

*I*N THE BEGINNING THERE WERE MEN WHO SIMPLY SAID,
'I am not going to buy this wine because it's made by a
woman. I am not interested in it.'" Marketta Fourmeaux, the
owner and winemaker of Château Potelle Winery, says this
matter-of-factly, without bitterness or anger in her voice. This is not
to say it didn't hurt her to release her lovingly, arduously crafted,
groundbreaking zinfandel of the 1980s while she remained in the
shadows—it did.

But there's a fine elegance to Marketta, a beautiful strength as
tough and lovely as the hillsides where she grows her vines. These
qualities are reflected in her wines. She never wore her disappoint-
ment on her sleeve, although no one could have blamed her if she
had.

"We said, 'Yeah, it's better for our brand if I stay quiet,' which I was never happy about because I thought it was unfair—but it was the way it was. At the beginning, one of the reasons that I didn't step up was that it would have been harmful for the brand."

Twenty years ago, this was the way it was when she and her now ex-husband and partner, Jean-Noel, left Paris for California. "It's never an easy thing to work as husband and wife. Our roles had to be very well defined, and my husband wanted it that way. Also, for the family, it was important that I stayed more in the background. I really began to come much more to the front line when the children were grown up and away at college. We had given them the education and home that we both wanted to give, and then I began to come more out from just being behind the scenes, the winemaker."

Marketta isn't standing on the sidelines anymore. Today, she is front and center at her two labels, Château Potelle in Napa and Gravity Hills in Paso Robles. Seeing this change in herself, as well as in the industry at large, has been a long time coming. "You know, since then, being a female winemaker or a woman in wine is actually very positive, because the women have stepped up. Today I go out there and people say, 'Oh, we love you. We love your wines. We want you! We want Château Potelle. We want to know more about you.' You know, it's just the opposite."

The odd thing is that this kind of gender discrimination wasn't limited to professionals in the industry. Marketta noticed it in her customers, too. Although, she notes, that's also changed, thankfully. "Women are more and more saying what they buy [at the winery]. You know, more and more we hear husbands say, 'Well, I'll take that, but what do you want; what do you like?' And the women are stepping up and saying, 'No, I like the chardonnay or I like the zin or I like whatever; I want that.' I think women, both as winemakers and as chefs, have a different sensitivity to flavors and combinations, which is really interesting. Women have more finesse in many ways and more delicate taste."

Marketta Fourmeaux

*W*hile Marketta loves a good classic food and wine pairing, she's adamant about not limiting oneself to hard and fast rules. "There is absolutely a truth that wines complement certain types of food, but it shouldn't be an issue. About every four years, I make a late-harvest zinfandel, a sweet wine. The other day, just for the heck of it, I made a roasted chicken with herbs. Just plain, very, very simple herbs and pasta, and I had it with this late harvest, sweet zinfandel. It was fantastic, and this is apparently as wrong as you can get it! So, indeed there is a truth, a foundation, in why certain wines go with certain foods—but don't stick to that. You know, explore, innovate, and search for what you enjoy."

It was Marketta's finesse that led her to take a chance on a craggy hilltop full of old zinfandel vines when everyone else was focused on cabernets in the Napa Valley.

From Paris to the Pacific

Like many kids growing up, Marketta had a fiercely independent streak and wanted to make her mark in the world, while stepping out of the first shadow she found herself in—her dad's. "I was born in Finland, and half of my childhood was in Helsinki in Finland and half was in Paris, so I grew up in two very different cultures. My father was a scientist; he was actually a Ph.D. in chemistry and geology who traveled a lot. I wanted to do something completely different." While in school, Marketta ended up with the same chemistry professor who had taught her dad many years earlier. "He kept saying, 'Oh, you should do like your father, you should do like your father,' and I got so sick and tired of hearing it. I decided that I was going to do something as far as I could find from science and chemistry." That turned out not to be a career involving wine, but getting an M.B.A. in marketing and business administration.

She and Jean-Noel met in Paris when Marketta was sixteen and he was seventeen. While he, too, would earn an M.B.A., they both had a passion for wine that couldn't be denied. "Part of his family is in production in Bordeaux, and we got very involved in the wine business. We had three businesses in France, all related to wine and food, but not the making of it." Marketta took her penchant for chemistry that she'd abandoned a few years earlier and applied it to her new passion, earning an enology degree in France and learning more from hands-on training at Jean-Noel's family business.

Meanwhile, Marketta and Jean-Noel landed jobs as official wine tasters for the Appellation d'Origine Controlée (AOC) in Bordeaux and in 1980 were sent on an unofficial trip to California to see whether the region's wine was indeed becoming a force to be reckoned with. "The wine has to be at a certain level, but it also has to be in a certain style, and we were among the people who tasted these wines before they actually were bottled. In 1980, we in Europe, we knew that something was going on; that California was developing as serious grape-growing country, but we didn't know on what level or where it fit in the global market at that time. We came in 1980, Jean-Noel and myself, and we stayed here over six months and tasted more than two thousand California wines, all the north grows, the central grows, the Monterey County. And, as we like to say, our report back to Bordeaux said, 'Looks good, we stay!'"

For Marketta and Jean-Noel, California was a land of exciting new possibilities. "Since we left, France has accepted new grape-growing regions, but we had nothing of that there at that time. So, frankly, it was pretty boring. And we are both kind of independent thinkers, and we wanted to do it our way. And obviously, France was not open for women in wine at that time, either. It just wasn't. I mean, I left France twenty years ago, but I know that now it's much, much, much, much easier." Things weren't much different in the States for women winemakers back then, either, but the less restrictive wine-production possibilities were enough to let Marketta turn the other cheek, for a little while, anyway. "We saw this opportunity in California, and it was crazy! We just looked at each other and said, 'How about it?' And then we decided to move."

The year was 1983, and Marketta and Jean-Noel had two small daughters by that time. Although they were starting from scratch, they did have friends in their new home. "I had been here in California as an exchange student with what they call A.S.S., the American Seal Service, in '68 and '69. And my host family actually was a vintner family. They had a vineyard in Dry Creek Valley in Hillsburg. I always loved them, and when we moved here, they really became our mom and dad. If somebody had told my older daughter that my 'American parents' were not her grandma and grandpa, she would have been furious!"

They settled into Menlo Park in Silicon Valley, where Marketta's American host family lived. "It was wonderful to have somebody here. We stayed there four and a half years, and that's the smartest thing we did." Still, their friends and family back home thought that the young couple had lost their minds. "We already own three companies, but they were too young so we didn't get much money when we sold them. And our family said, 'You guys are crazy, you have such a good life here! What are you doing?' And then, obviously, many said, 'Oh, why do you go to America? You know you can't make good wines in America!'"

At first, Marketta began to wonder if they'd been right. Not about the quality of the wines she knew she could make, but about the opportunities that were available. "Our idea was that we would not own any vineyards. We would have grape contractors, and I would make our blend, and we would have our selections and our own label. What we wanted to do is totally normal today, but at that time in California, the high-end consumer did not accept the idea that you did not own your vineyard and you did not actually own the building."

They poured all of their money into this initial idea—and, subsequently, lost it all. With two small kids to support, Marketta and

*I*n the 1930s, the major European wine-producing countries created a set of standards for grape growing in order to preserve regional culture and tradition. The laws, known as the appellation laws, dictate what grapes may be used to produce wine in particular regions. So, if you wanted to make cabernet sauvignon in Alsace instead of in Bordeaux, you'd be out of luck. Or, at least, you wouldn't be allowed to put the AOC stamp of approval on your label. New grape-growing regions have been accepted into the appellation laws over the years, but the laws are very strict and do not change quickly.

Jean-Noel needed to find a new way. "I remember there was one night in March. We stayed the whole night in the bathtub together, and all the way until midnight we were saying, 'What did we do wrong to fail? Why are we in this situation?' And then after midnight, we began to make a new plan. We started the next day. We had no money, but we had quite a bit of inventory." That's when they knew they needed to own their own winery. But with all of their money gone, they had to think way out of the box.

"I think we could have a Nobel Prize in creative financing!" Marketta laughs. "You know, banks don't give you money when you need it. They give you money when you really don't need it anymore. So our first hint of investors were friends of my American dad. And, you know, we were talking very little money. But then we grew from there."

It took four years before they found their first property, a vineyard on the Silverado Trail in Calistoga. "We knew exactly the style of wine that we wanted to make, so we put a lot of effort into finding the place. There was one piece of land; it was so cheap, but mind you, we didn't have a penny. But we had to buy it, and we signed the contract. Then we said, 'Okay, now we bought it—where's the money?'

"I have always been the brains of our business; I am the wine and the vineyard and a very good chunk of the business thinking. My husband has been the business sales, and he is very good in sales, very charismatic." That charisma led them to some investors who would fund the initial operation. A year and a half later, they sold the Calistoga vineyard for double its initial price, and in 1988, they found the property on Mount Veeder in Napa that would become Château Potelle.

"When we bought on Mount Veeder, nobody wanted to be on the mountain. Nobody! But we have always been a little bit ahead in our thinking. When we first came here, the Americans were not sensitive to vineyards. We were surprised it was all about the wine-maker. You know, the winemaker was the magical hand that could transfer grapes into fine wine, so the raw material was not an issue, nor was style."

The industry was very young back then, but many vineyards were also being bought up as tax shelters by moneyed people outside of the wine industry. "At that time, most of the vineyards in Napa Valley were owned by lawyers and doctors. They didn't know anything about the business, so they planted whatever, however, wherever, whereas we came from hundreds of years of trial and error in vine-yard planting. Back home, it was just common knowledge that the vineyard makes the wine. Of course, you need a very talented wine-maker, but if you don't have good grapes to start with, I don't care what your talent is, you can make a very good wine, but you cannot make a great wine."

The Zin That Changed It All

The Mount Veeder property was formerly a 202-acre cattle ranch, but the prior owner had dabbled a bit in grape growing. "He planted the initial vineyards in the 1960s, so we had all the vines there. There's less topsoil on the hillside. The ground is poor compared to the valley soil, which is rich. But the vine is kind of a desert plant. It really gives the best of itself when it has to struggle a little bit."

Those old, struggling vines became Marketta's muse. "When we came to America, zinfandel wine had no value. It was like the poor man's cabernet that you had with spaghetti and meatballs. We tasted some zinfandel, and we said, 'This is a phenomenal wine,' but it was often made in a way that we wouldn't have made it. Our property on Mount Veeder had five acres of wonderful old-vine zin, and I told Jean-Noel, 'Look, you know what I am going to do. I am going to make these grapes in the same fashion that we would be making the most expensive cabernet in Bordeaux, and let's see what it can do.' And we did!

"The wine just became absolutely wonderful, and then we decided to package it completely differently and doubled the price of anybody else on the market. The wine really became what you would call a cult wine very fast."

The success of Château Potelle spurred them on to look for another piece of property. Marketta wanted to make another zinfandel, but because she knew that where a grape is grown is as important as who works with the end product, she set out looking in other zin-friendly areas. "We wanted to make another zin, so we began to look for other regions that were traditional zin counties, like Amador County, Dry Creek Valley, and Paso Robles. In 1995, we found the land, the climate, and the soil in Paso." Their timing once again was perfect. "Two years after we invested, the prices doubled and tripled. Currently, we have two hundred ninety acres in Paso."

The acreage in Paso Robles consisted of a dying almond orchard on a hillside. Marketta and Jean-Noel pulled out all the stops—they brought in all their machinery and manpower to turn the orchard into a vineyard in 1996. "We had to house all our men from Napa there for six months to be able to start the vineyard, but there was nobody else [doing this back then]." It has more than paid off.

"We make twenty-five thousand cases combined from Mount Veeder and the Paso Robles property. We really changed the way

*W*here does the name Château Potelle come from? "When we left France, we left everything. We felt like taking something with us that was really deep, deeply rooted in the family, in the culture. Château Potelle is a thousand-year-old family château that comes from the family of my mother-in-law, and it's been in this single family for five hundred years."

Americans think about zinfandel." Eventually, Marketta also changed how the wine industry and its fans looked at women winemakers, and at no small cost. It's not every person who can uproot her life and find a new one in an unfamiliar country, to go from penniless to successful on sheer ingenuity and drive.

As is sometimes the way, the success has a bittersweet flavor. Their vineyards thrived, as did their two daughters, who have grown up and pursued their own interests, just as Marketta wanted to when she was young. Her marriage to Jean-Noel, though, suffered under the strain.

"The only thing is, it cost our marriage. We just divorced, and that's the very, very sad part. Our divorce got final actually in December 2005, and now we are learning to become friends rather than husband and wife. And that is working, actually. I think we both are very happy like this, but it's just, you know . . . it's just sad. I think it is often when you get married really young, and then family takes over and business takes over, and you kind of never matured your own relationship. And then, all of a sudden, you wake up in the morning and you say, 'Hey, we don't share things anymore.' It was very hard for both of us and the children, too. But now even our children say, 'Well, look, we prefer to see you both happy as you are than married if it didn't work.'"

So now, Marketta, at age fifty-two, has once again found herself in new territory. Life on her own is a bit like planting that vineyard on a hilltop—difficult, sure, but the best fruit can't be harvested without a little toil. And lately, the long-dormant words of her mother have been resurrected in her mind.

"When I was a young girl, I was very talented academically and everything, but I remember one thing my mother always used to always tell me. She said, 'You know, I don't want you to hear that you can't do anything, because you can do everything you want. The only question is, are you willing to put in the time it takes to do it?' So I never grew up thinking that I couldn't do something."

8

HEIDI PETERSON BARRETT

Winemaker, Screaming Eagle and La Sirena

> I personally measure success in terms of the contributions an
> individual makes to her or his fellow human beings.
>
> —Margaret Mead, *Redbook*, 1978

*T*IME MAGAZINE REFERS TO HER AS THE WINE DIVA OF
Napa. And point-wielding Robert Parker tipped his hat by
proclaiming her the First Lady of Wine, as well as awarding
four of her wines 100-point marks. With such well-earned
accolades, you'd think Heidi Peterson Barrett might (deservedly!)
have a bit of a swagger at this point in her winemaking career.

Rather than acting like the national wine treasure that Heidi is,
she acts more like a kid who just won first prize at her local science
fair.

"You definitely kind of smile to yourself and float around on
cloud nine for the day when those reviews come out. But I'm mostly
just really grateful that I do well in the business. And there are just
so many little things along the way that are very gratifying and that
you feel really good about if you've done something special. Or

being able to have your wine go to people whom it can help. It's through the charity work, the wines that I make for charity auctions, that's a really fun thing for me, too. I think just the day-to-day smaller accomplishments are often what really mean the most. It's more that kind of thing instead of one big stand-out moment."

You could attribute this to the notion that Heidi has grown up around the wine industry—it's all kind of second nature for her. The lauding that comes along with it? To her, those are the momentary perks in a lifetime commitment. And yet you also get a sense that Heidi can't quite believe that she's the one critics are talking about.

"I keep 'Peterson,'" she says, in explanation of her double last name, "because a lot of people know me because my dad was also a winemaker. Since there are no sons, I pretty much carry on winemaking in our family."

After twenty-five years in the business, Heidi certainly doesn't need any extra introductions, but family is something that she takes as seriously as her calling in life. Whether it's as a working mom or as the daughter who carries the good family name into the next generation of the wine industry, she's up for the challenge. Yet even with the Peterson golden seal of approval, it hasn't always been easy.

"I think my name helped me to get hired, but then I was kind of on my own. I think I could have easily dropped the ball and gotten myself fired, too, if I didn't do a good job for people. That was a good foot in the door, but then I pretty much had to pick up the ball on my own and go with it. Early on, every time I would take a different job, there was always this sort of trial period where you'd have to prove yourself over and over and over."

Certainly, as a working mom, she did not have it easy. "Juggling having children with work is a big challenge. I think most women can relate to that. I pretty much worked very, very part time when my girls were really young. And I worked from home a lot as much as I could. Then, as they got a little older and started school, I was able to take on a little more work.

"I was full time at Buehler Vineyards when I married my

Heidi Peterson Barrett

husband, Bo [who is the winemaker at Château Montelena]. For a while, they let me bring the babies to work. I think that ultimately, they thought they'd rather have somebody who didn't have all that, though, so I left to do freelance, which was actually a godsend."

In more ways than one: not only did it allow her to raise her daughters, now seventeen and nineteen, but that freelance work turned out to be the thing that would set her apart—the work she did as a winemaker for both Dalle Valle Vineyards and Screaming Eagle earned her the two 100-point Robert Parker ratings at each winery. One wine even went for a half million dollars at the 2000 Napa Valley Wine Auction, and now she's even got her wine label, La Sirena.

"It actually kind of happened on a fluke. The wine for La Sirena first started as a custom crush wine that I had made for a client, who hired me to make a sangiovese for them." The client, who was from a larger winemaking family, was none too pleased that some of its members were branching off and making a competing wine. "Their family kind of gave them the ultimatum that either you stick with us or you're out, so they decided they couldn't finish the project. They were going to put this beautiful wine on the bulk market. I thought it was really delicious stuff, and I kind of thought for the first time, 'Well, maybe I could buy it from them, and this could be my chance to start my label.'"

She did. Yet believe it or not, with all this under her belt, there was a time when Heidi didn't have a clue she would take this path.

The Great Fate

"You know, I didn't know this was what I'd end up doing. And here I'd been visiting all these wineries all my life, and it was just so much a normal part of our world. I'd been tasting wine since I was probably two! It was just always around. My dad would bring home different things that he was working on and say, "Taste this wine; what do you think about this? What does it taste like to you?"

Even though she was learning about wine from her scientist-winemaker dad, Heidi didn't realize that she was training her palate for her future career. "I really wasn't even thinking what I was going to do until the last minute, senior year, when people started asking, 'Where are you going to go to college? What do you want to be when you grow up?' I was like, well, I've already been working in the winery. That was always my summer job as a kid, in high school, and I'd work in the vineyard or the cellar. I really enjoyed it. I pretty much only applied at U.C. Davis in the winemaking department. I got in, and I never looked back."

As Dr. Ann Noble's (see chapter 14) assistant at U.C. Davis, Heidi began to take seriously what she'd been around her entire life, her father was a huge influence on her future. "I think I was really fortunate that I kind of got dropped on the planet in a winemaking family, because I wonder whether I would have found this if I had

---

After spending time as Dr. Ann Noble's assistant, Heidi got to work firsthand with the Wine Aroma Wheel (see chapter 1) and still uses it to this day. "It's just such a great tool. It really simplifies the whole flavor profile. If you look at the wheel, there's a section that has maybe all the red fruit characteristics versus black fruit characteristics—herbal qualities, spiciness, and all those things. For me, I love looking at it, and sometimes I'll even use it when I write my tasting notes. As a guide, it really helps me define what the flavors are. And you're able to train your brain a little bit better how to remember wine, and what are the flavors that you actually do like and can then look for. I just think it's really handy."

---

been born into something else. I don't know how other people happen upon it. It seems like it would be a great stroke of luck or some sort of destiny."

Heidi's destiny brought her family to Modesto.

"I was born in Berkeley when my dad was in the Ph.D. program there and getting his degree in agricultural chemistry. At the time, there wasn't a winemaking department, so that was as close as you could get. I was born in '57, so in '58, he was out of school and got hired by Gallo in Modesto to be in charge of new product development. He was their research director. It was really fun for him, and he got to experiment a lot and create new products for them, and I think it was just a dream job for him at the time. He stayed for ten years.

"In the late '50s, early '60s, there weren't very many wineries around at that time. It was well before the big California wine boom in the early '70s, when there was just kind of an explosion of new brands taking off in Napa Valley. At that time, early on, there was just a handful of the bigger producers. The Paris Tasting hadn't happened yet, where California wines just burst onto the scene. But it was fun for my sister and me. My dad took us to work, and it was this huge factory. We just thought that was fascinating as kids, to see the whole production line thing, even the making of their own glass."

Where does one of America's preeminent winemakers like to dine? "I love Don Giovanni. It's really fun. It's an Italian restaurant in Napa, in Yountville. Oh, and Angele! That's a good restaurant. It's just up the street from the Napa Valley Opera House, about four blocks. You can go hear music or see whatever show they have and then head over to Angele for dinner. It's a really fun little outing!"

After a decade at Gallo, Heidi's dad left Modesto in 1968 and headed to Napa to become the winemaker at Beaulieu Vineyard, and even though he would eventually relocate his family to Monterey, it was Napa that would bring Heidi closer to her destiny. "It just always felt like home to me."

So much so that it's where she's settled today. "I live out in the country in a little town ten minutes north of Calistoga at the north end of the Napa Valley. We live on the side of the hill, at the foot of Mount Saint Helena. We have a couple of waterfalls that just flow right by our house—right in our yard practically is this one huge waterfall. It's just spectacular, and the sound of it's incredible. And there are a bunch of caves. You can hike up in the mountain. It's really pretty. I have eight clients within four different locations, so everything is within a half hour of my house. I love it."

Rolling Up Her Sleeves

There was a bit of a road to travel between Heidi's days at U.C. Davis and her becoming one of the most sought-out winemakers in Napa. Often, she was the odd woman out.

"That's really changed, through my career from when I started. There were so few women in the business, but now it's become really commonplace. There are so many women coming out of U.C. Davis and similar winemaking schools now. Even around the world—the strides that have been made in the last, even twenty, years are remarkable. I think about the year that I graduated from U.C. Davis. It was 1980, and there were thirty graduates; only four of them were women. And of those four, I think only two actually went on to become winemakers. I don't know what the percentage is now, but I think it's a little closer to almost fifty-fifty."

Maybe because her winemaker dad had always encouraged her, or maybe because it was her nature not to be held back, but Heidi never let the odds intimidate her. "I'd often be the only woman out there, so I wore the men's work suits. At the Monterey Vineyard,

*Y*ou'd think Heidi wouldn't have much time for
anything else outside work and her family, but
she actually makes jewelry, paints, scuba dives, and
knits! The latter hobby has become a big family
favorite lately. "I hadn't done it in years and just kind
of got back into it a couple of years ago. I also knitted
when my kids were really young, and then I got really
busy so I gave it up for a long time, and then just
started again a couple of years ago and retaught my
girls, too. So, all three of us are into it." All of her
extra activities help explain why there is no TV in the
house. "I just don't have time," she says—although
she does make one exception: she watches the
Olympics every two years.

this one guy was about my same size, so I borrowed his; we both
wore the same one. You know, it's pretty funny. But I never let it
hold me back. I didn't even expect that it ever would hold me back.
I just worked really hard, and I think [the men] respected that. I
worked right alongside everybody. I volunteered and jumped right
in and did anything. So it just became kind of a normal part of the
cellar. That was maybe part of the key, that it never even crossed my
mind that there would be a problem, and there wasn't."

Heidi's own experiences—which included raising independent,
confident daughters—did come from the foundation she was given
by her own parents, and she's quick to credit them as the force
behind her own independent nature. "I think the way that our parents raised us was to let us know that you can pursue whatever your
interests are, and you have the possibility of being really successful
at it if you love what you do and you just dive right in. So it never
was even brought to my attention that I wouldn't be able to be a
winemaker because I happen to be a woman."

The funny thing is, Heidi got a lot more raised eyebrows in the tasting rooms than in the cellar. "I used to get it a lot more. I might be at a tasting and pouring the wine, and people would ask, 'Oh, do you work at the winery?' and I'd say, 'Yeah,' and they'd ask, 'Oh, are you in marketing?' and I'd say, 'No, I'm the winemaker.' And their jaws would kind of drop."

For her, though, this was always a fun exercise in shaking things up. "I used to love surprising people that way, especially if they always just assumed you did sales, or you worked in the tasting room. They always asked, 'How did you get into that?' They wanted to know more. Often, they didn't even realize it was a possibility that women could become winemakers. That was always fun, just to have that surprise and open a few eyes to the possibilities of the job."

The Not-So-Simple Life

The biggest misconceptions Heidi deals with these days have more to do with just being a plain old winemaker, regardless of whether she is a man or a woman. Far from having a cushy job, she's busy 365 days a year. But oddly, it's a fact of the winemaking life that not many people seem to know about. "Everyone thinks we drink a lot," she says, laughing. "They think, 'Oh, sure, you just get to drink all day!' I hear that and it's like, wow, I hardly ever drink. I taste a lot, but I spit them all out. And when I come home at the end of the day, sometimes the last thing I want is a glass of wine."

She's also surprised that people often assume that most of her year is spent sitting by the pool, and that the only time a winemaker needs to really dig in is during harvest. Nothing could be farther from the truth. "People sometimes think we only really work during the crush, that once the grapes are harvested, then we must have nothing else to do. But every season there's something going on. Every month it's different; there's always a lot of work to do in every phase of the wine.

"Once you get the grapes picked, it's only the beginning of our work. Then you actually make wine and are fine-tuning the wine, and blending, and you're bottling, and you're ordering barrels for the following year, you're ordering bottling supplies, you do sales, you do wine tastings, you do all kinds of stuff; and the whole process of clarifying the wine, and all kinds of steps that go on all the rest of the year—I think people aren't aware of it."

So what's a typical day like for her? "It just really depends on the week. I had bottling on Monday for one of my clients, so I got some zinfandel bottled up for them. That was a busy day. The next day I had a radio interview. Sometimes I have big winery work, more marketing stuff, and I don't have a lot of time do to that, because I really need to be troubleshooting and making sure there are no problems."

While some people wouldn't like the unpredictable nature of her work, it fits her to a tee. "The flexibility of it, the way I've structured it, I just set my own schedule. Like today, I'm able to stay home and get work done from here, which is awesome. Tomorrow I'm going to go to the cellar, and I have a big blending day. It's not a time clock–puncher type of job at all, which I love. Sometimes I'm out in the vineyard. Sometimes I'm in the lab. Sometimes I'm in the cellar. Sometimes I'm at a trade tasting. It is a lot of work, and it's a bit of a juggling act some days, trying to fit everything in, but I really love that about it."

With all that juggling, it makes you wonder how she manages to produce so many unique wines for each of her clients. How does she do it? "The vineyards are so, so different that the winemaking will also be customized to match each of those vineyards. The wine is mostly determined by the grapes that I have available and the vineyards producing a lot of great fruit to work with. But beyond that, I'll look at any given property and try to figure out what's got the best potential. What's the best wine we can make with what we have to work with here? It's kind of more about bringing their fruit to life versus imprinting my style on it. And yet my style comes through no matter what, because it's just how I go about making

*H*eidi's take on dressing for the job: "You wear jeans, pretty much, and just stuff you can work in. But we also need to look good because we are women. I usually wear lipstick." Heidi laughs. "I do! I wear a little bit of makeup. But I try to find lipstick that doesn't have any smell or taste to it, which is a little bit of a weird thing to look for. And nothing too bright, but just a little bit so I feel a little bit put together."

wine. When you line up the different wines that I make, there is a lot of similarity in the balance and the richness and silkiness of the wine, but the fruit character will vary greatly. Plus, then you bring in the vintage differences. There's no way they could taste the same. All my clients just trust me to do a great job for them and get the work done. The way I go about it is up to me." That's just how Heidi likes it.

9

STEPHANIE BROWNE
Founder of Divas Uncorked

Passion is energy. Feel the power that comes
from focusing on what excites you.

—Oprah Winfrey

YOU WILL HEAR A LOT OF PEOPLE IN THIS BOOK TALK
about passion. When you're discussing a topic as intoxicating
as wine, it's pretty easy to get carried away with it. For
Stephanie Browne, she's gotten so carried away with her passion for vino, she's made it her second job. But for the founder of Divas
Uncorked—a ten-woman wine group that has motivated the creation
of countless clubs all over the country—who is also an advocate for
women and people of color nationwide, she's just getting started.

"I leave my regular job and I work another eight hours on Divas.
I probably am working sixteen hours a day and every weekend,
too," Stephanie says. And it all started with dinner.

"Back in 1999, I was friends with probably half of the group. I
worked with them in a nonprofit organization, and we used to
always go out and have dinner after our meetings, and that is where

I started to gain an interest in wine. We would order wine with dinner, and I found out during that process of drinking wine that I didn't know a heck of a lot. Most of the time I would order a glass of white wine or a glass of red wine. I didn't really ask for a particular type, I just usually ordered the house wine—I wasn't even savvy enough to know that there were different types of red house wines!"

The more Stephanie realized how much there was to learn, the more she wanted to know, and thus Divas Uncorked—the group whose motto is "Wine savvy, not wine snobby"—was born. "I wanted to know more, but I wasn't comfortable just experimenting without any kind of information to understand what I was doing, so I asked a group of a few women that I was dining with, 'Hey, why don't we start a wine club?' I was not new to Boston, but Boston is kind of a strange city. It is pretty cliquish from a friendship perspective, and so I was always looking to meet other folks." With that, Stephanie asked her six friends, all African American women, to each bring another friend into the fold in order to expand their social circle and learn a little more about wine.

Stephanie loves that the American experience with wine is becoming more akin to the way Europeans include it in their lives every day. "I think wine has become very much part of the day-to-day culinary experience, and because of that, people are a lot more interested. If I want it as part of my culinary experience, I need to know at least enough about it so that I can make sure that I have a good experience every time I partake in it. And the whole culinary experience has greatly changed in America over the last five to ten years. We are becoming much more diverse in what we will try."

Stephanie Browne

"There were really only two premises: one, that you hosted once a year; and two, that every time you brought us together, there was a form of education. We weren't just tasting, then; that way we would build our knowledge and our palates."

They were also discovering something else—that there was no reason to be intimidated by wine. A whole delicious world of grapes lay out there just waiting to be plucked, so to speak. The more Stephanie thought about it, the more she saw that women—and minority women, in particular—were missing out, and for no good reason. "It has been a snobby, unapproachable thing for so many years except for, you know, the jug wine. But even though there are jug wines, there still are some good jug wines! You just need to learn more about them."

That was when the Divas became a force to be reckoned with.

Wine for All, and All for Wine

The Divas began to notice that wine snobbery started in the marketing of wine, something Stephanie has learned quite a bit about in her day job as a telecommunications director. She approached several wineries about forming a partnership to help them aim their sights at women and people of color.

"A lot of what we are doing with the winery partnerships definitely has to do with the fact that we want them to recognize there is an eighty-billion-dollar marketplace from an African American perspective. The second is having them understand what it is to market to people of color, and not just to the African American market. We are helping them to understand what the cultural differences are, which, from a marketing perspective, will help them reach that different market segment."

One aspect, Stephanie notes, relates to cultural traditions in the kitchen. "A lot of that has to do with what is different from a cultural food perspective, and what do we want to see in the companies that market to us? What are the things that are important to us as a demographic group? We are helping our partners from that perspective."

Her marketing prowess comes at a cost, though—a socially conscious one. So far, the Diva wine partners are all getting on board. "We work with our partners on their social and community initiatives. One of our requirements for partnering with any of the wineries or any of the businesses within the wine chain is that they work with us on what they are doing from a social community perspective. Most of them have something going on, but we try to get them to understand how you determine what the need is and then build your policies and your programs around the need, as opposed to doing only the things that are visible and not necessarily addressing the needs that are in your community or where your biggest target base is.

"So, if you want to expand in Massachusetts or in New York, what are you doing in New York and Massachusetts to let the public know who you are and what you are and what you are all about

---

*W*hat's Stephanie's favorite pairing? "I love to cook, and I love enchiladas! I lived in the Southwest for about ten years, in Tucson, Arizona. I was nineteen, so I still needed a mother at that time, and I had this wonderful woman who actually worked with me who became like an adopted mother to me. She taught me how to cook Mexican style. I make wonderful enchiladas now—and I like enchiladas with Viognier. It is originally a grape from France, but it's all over the world now. It is very fruity—apricot, apple, almost passion fruit–based—but it is not real sweet. It pairs very well with tomato-based things."

---

from a social message perspective? Instead of saying 'My wine is good,' let's say, 'My whole company is good, and this is why you ought to buy my brand.'"

Stephanie and the Divas have also been working with their wine partners on career development opportunities for women and people of color. "We've worked with a couple of our partners to build scholarships and internships so that we can at least start to fill some of those entry-level jobs with folks who can now build their repertoire and their résumé, and hopefully someday get to the top of the house—so that the organization has some diversity.

"It was always presumed that the service industry was low paying and hard work. I would say it is probably still hard work, but I think the low-paying aspect is changing because it can now be a career versus just a job. More and more people are going to the culinary schools, which are now obviously teaching a lot about wine, and going through programs that are designed for the hospitality indus-

Divas Uncorked

try. A lot of big service industry companies like the Starwoods and the Marriotts are looking for career-oriented individuals versus just service individuals."

You can see how Stephanie needs an extra eight hours a day to keep up with what's become her second job. Her enthusiasm and passion for it are so great that she makes you think that change isn't just possible, it's happening right now. "I get a daily e-mail from winejobs.com, and there are tons of jobs that don't require you to have three years of wine industry background. You get in at entry level and you learn. And you never know, you might be that next African American or Mexican American winery owner, or you might just want to be the VP of marketing in one of these big wineries!"

Sisters Sipping It Over

Despite all of the great work they are doing to open up the world of wine to U.S. women of all colors, the Divas haven't forgotten their original impetus: learning, enjoying, and sipping. At this point, the Divas have started an annual wine conference for women and its own wine label. ("We are working with Mendocino Wine Company to build a private label for Divas.") The group has also started to sponsor wine education dinners called Diva Dine, where fifty to seventy-five women gather for an evening of wine education and fun.

"We want other women to replicate what we do around the country so we have created what we call a network. A lot of people were asking us, 'How did you get started? What did you do? How did you formalize? How did you create structure around it?' So we have made a PDF download available on our Web site that talks about the whole concept and how we got started. We primarily focused on California wines in the beginning because they are easy to learn, then you can venture off and try Italy and France and all the rest of the world. But we felt that for brand-new, beginning people right out of the gate, it is much easier to learn with a California wine where the wine is named by the varietal. It is easy to understand where the winery is and what the winery is all about based on the way the packaging is done."

When all is said and sipped, though, Stephanie's mission goes beyond race, culture, and equality. The common denominator is connecting. And if that's done through wine? All the better.

"I think the whole notion of sisterhood, friendship, making sure you take advantage of life in general might have stemmed a lot out of 9/11. You know, life is real short. You don't realize it until something that catastrophic happens, and it makes you aware that friends are really valuable, and you shouldn't be too busy to spend time with your loved ones. Finding ways to get together and enjoy each other is really important in life.

"I think what I would love to be able to do with Divas Uncorked is five years from now to have created a paradigm shift in the way that the industry thinks about the marketplace when it comes to women and people of color. When I started out becoming a wine enthusiast, there were obstacles, and I would love to be able to remove all of those obstacles for the next person coming behind me. When you look at wine magazines like *Food & Wine* and *Bon Appetit*, I want you to see a diverse population that matches and mirrors what the real population in America is. And that we are *all* enjoying great food and great wine every single day. That would be my ultimate dream. It is still early in the game, very early in the game."

Knowing Stephanie, I suspect that her dream won't remain one for too long.

10

MERRY EDWARDS

Winemaker, Merry Edwards Wines

The fruit that can fall without shaking,
Indeed is too mellow for me.

—Lady Mary Wortley Montagu

WHICH COMES FIRST: THE FOOD OR THE GRAPE? And do winemakers think about food when they make wine? It's an interesting question to mull over. Some do; some don't. In the case of the ever-fascinating Merry Edwards, a winemaker and the owner of her namesake wines and vineyard, the two sensual delights are not mutually exclusive. It was her passion for the kitchen that foretold her life in the vineyard.

"I had taught myself how to cook in high school and kind of became the cook for my family. I had a lady I babysat for who was a fantastic cook, and she taught me how to bake bread and pies from scratch. My mom didn't like cooking back then, but my family really liked my cooking. By the time I graduated from high school, I was cooking four nights a week, and I enjoyed it."

As luck would have it, Merry stumbled upon her first glimpse of the fusion between her two passions right in her own home. "I had started digging through the cookbooks that my mom had, and I found two that were published by the California Wine Institute. Of course, every recipe had wine. My parents had to go out and buy wine for me to put in those recipes because they didn't drink. I introduced my parents to wine."

Today, Merry's parents are proud supporters of their talented daughter's accomplishments and career. "I have a small corporation; my husband and my parents are two of my shareholders. My mom is eighty-six and my dad is eighty-eight. My dad still enjoys some wine, but my mom really doesn't drink much of anything anymore."

It wasn't always like this. "My parents helped me when I was an undergraduate, but once I hit graduate school, I was pretty much on my own. I actually wanted to become a veterinarian, but I didn't get much support for that idea. My dad really wanted me to become a dental hygienist."

Before you gasp in horror, consider the time: the women's movement was in its early stages, and the idea that parents should send their daughters off to college was still a bit of a novelty. More and more women were in the workforce, but for the average middle-class parent, trade school was a popular direction for female children. For women in the wine industry, the job of the day was lab technician—but we'll get to that a little later in Merry's story.

"My parents just had one marriage between them, but a lot of their friends were getting divorced at the time. I mean, a lot of them! So my dad was talking to me as though I already had two kids and I needed a job to support them after I was divorced. That's the kind of mentality he had when I was in college."

Still, Merry wasn't keen on the idea of becoming a dental hygienist, despite her father's attempts to convince her of its practicality. "I had the idea that I wanted to become a nurse. I chose Berkeley to go to school and started off aiming for nursing, but then along the way decided that it really wasn't what I wanted to do." Instead,

Merry Edwards

Merry earned a degree in physiology. After graduating, she and her boyfriend decided to move to Washington, just outside of Seattle.

"After I went up to Washington State, I started cooking and making everything I could think of out of the local fruit: muffins and ice cream and canning blackberry jam." That was Merry's pivotal moment.

"I thought, 'I wonder if you could make wine out of these berries?' So I went to the Tacoma City library and checked out a book on home winemaking, but I was too broke to even buy the minimal equipment that you would need to make wine at home." Lacking money, Merry stayed in Tacoma during that summer and used her background in science to get a job with a local doctor. "I basically had followed a pre-med curriculum, but I had no degree I could really do anything practical with. I didn't want to do research.

"I moved back to Berkeley, and got a job as a lab tech." In the meantime, Merry was still trying to forge a career path and went back to school to get her master's in nutrition from Berkeley. "I thought, I have to go back to school and get some other kind of credentials."

Wise words from Merry, a wise woman: "I think that people should remember that they are the judge; they shouldn't be intimidated by what anybody else says. What amuses me is that people are so intimidated by wine that they think that somebody else should tell them what to drink. If you have a steak, do you let someone else decide whether the steak is good or bad? You taste the steak and you say, 'I like this steak,' or 'I don't like this steak.' People should be the same way with wine. I make several different pinots. You may not like all of them, but there's going to be one that you're going to love. You are the judge."

Merry began making wine and beer at home just for the fun of it. "All of my friends enjoyed the products I was making, but they would have probably drunk anything back then, right?" She laughs. "Then I met Andy Quady, who owns Quady Port Works down in Madera. They specialize in and just make dessert wines. He was going to U.C. Davis studying winemaking, and I had no idea that it was so scientific. I thought it was like an art."

The more Merry talked with Andy about his program of study, the more excited she became. "He said, 'Why don't you come visit the school?' So I went to Davis and saw the pilot plant there and talked to a lot of the teachers, and I was fascinated by the whole thing."

Still, she didn't exactly have a trust fund to send herself to graduate school. Despite the urging of the Viticulture and Enology Department head, Merry knew her financial limits and assumed that it was a nice dream, but she'd have to be satisfied with taking books out of the library and making wine at home. Then the head of the department at U.C. Davis offered her a scholarship.

"The school had no women in the department—there were two other women in my class—and they were looking for women, so I took them up on it." A year and a half later, she obtained her master's degree in enology from the country's most prestigious and respected wine program. Merry made history as one of the first few women after pioneer Mary Ann Graf to graduate from the program, and of the three women classmates in the program, she is the only one who became a winemaker.

The Grapes of Wrath

The welcome that Merry received at U.C. Davis couldn't have prepared her for what would come afterward. Today, as many of the winemakers I've talked with for this book can attest, women make up a significant part of the industry—and not just in the traditional lab technician jobs. In the 1970s, when California's wine revolution was beginning, it was a different story.

*M*erry has a fundamental tip about wine and food pairing: "I think people shouldn't get too hung up with what goes with what. There are two basic ways chefs look at pairing wine with food. There is the like-like philosophy or the contrast philosophy. You may taste a wine and look for the elements that are similar to the dish you are cooking, which would be a like-like. An example is mushrooms and pinot noir—pinot noir has a nice, earthy, forest floor, mushroom, fungal thing going on, so that's why it goes so well with mushrooms. The other thing you can do is to contrast the wine with something to set it off, and that's the other way chefs look at pairing.

"I think, however, that more people feel comfortable with bringing out a flavor that's already there, rather than trying to come up with something that will be more of a startling comparison."

"It was the early '70s, and even though there was not supposed to be discrimination in hiring, especially in the universities, they had a system at Davis where the industry would send in letters to the department to whatever professor they liked. Those professors would then turn around and, instead of posting the letters as general notices in the department, they would just pass them along to a favorite student.

"One of the big companies from New Zealand came in. I was young and single and I thought, New Zealand would be great! So I went to the chairman of the department and said, 'I'd like to be in on this interview,' and the chairman of the department said I couldn't. And when I asked why not, he said because they won't hire women in New Zealand."

Merry was indignant, and rightfully so. The notion that a company would discriminate against an entire gender was outrageous. "I said, 'Why is the university hosting a hiring day for a company that will not hire women—and you have three women graduates in this class?' He wouldn't back down, so I went to the university's hiring department and told them this has to stop. They thought I was this big rabble-rouser, but I said, 'You accepted me to go to school here yet you're not going to support me in getting a job?'

"By then I had missed the interview with the New Zealand company, but after that, every professor had to disclose the letters or requests for employees and post them in the department so everyone could look at them."

Merry took a brave, independent stand, and the policy was forever changed at U.C. Davis, and in June 2005, "they invited me to

---

*W*hat's Merry's advice for gaining wine knowledge? "Go in and talk to a small shop owner. They get to know you, they get to know your taste, and they don't fixate on what you should like. What they need to do is find out what you do like so you come back and buy more of that. They can also turn you on to new things. But their job is to find something that you will actually buy and enjoy. Also, keep an eye out for local wine shops, or local vineyards if you have them, that offer tastings—it's a great way to learn more without investing a ton of money." Merry's winery offers tastings by appointment only—so be sure to call first if you're heading out to the Russian River Valley.

---

speak at their 125th anniversary. How times change." But it wasn't the last time she'd bump up against old-school ideas about who should be making wine.

"My given name is Meredith. On a résumé, some people may think Meredith Edwards is a man because it's actually an English name. It's not a very common name anyway. Sometimes I would be granted an interview, and then people would find out that I wasn't a guy. I went through quite a few discouraging experiences."

In fact, it happened so often that Merry could tell just by the look on the interviewer's face that he had been expecting a male candidate. "They would make it short, or sometimes they would cancel because if they called me on the phone, there was this silence when they figured that it was actually me, a woman, on the phone. I had some rather confrontational interviews. I would figure out about halfway through that they had absolutely no intention of hiring me, but they felt once I was there, they had to go through with it."

About ten minutes into an interview with one winery owner, Merry became exasperated with yet another glazed-eyed man who she could tell wasn't interested. So she confronted him. "I said to the owner of the winery, 'You really have no intention of hiring me, do you?' and he said, 'Absolutely not. There's no way I would hire a woman.'" Then the interviewer went on to describe his ideal candidate—something between Matthew McConaughey and George Clooney. "He wanted this young, studly guy who could basically bench press or something."

Her sense of humor notwithstanding, the ugly truth about women in the early stages of the California wine industry was that they weren't always a welcome addition to a winery. "I had another case where I went to the interview, and they said that there's no way I could do anything physical. When I told Dr. Maynard Amerine, who was my major professor at Davis and my mentor, he became upset. He called them and said, 'What are you doing with my protégée? She is incredible!' So they called back and offered me a job in the lab, and I said, 'You know, I don't want a job in the lab. I've

already done that. What I need is the winemaking in the cellar.'"
She turned them down.

A Vineyard of Her Own

For Merry, the ultimate goal is to grow, make, and sell her own
wines—something she tried but didn't succeed at the first time in
1984. Merry being Merry, however, she persevered and is the owner
of her own business today, Meredith Vineyard Estate, which she
founded in 1997 to make Merry Edwards Wines.

She certainly doesn't wear it on her sleeve, but she keeps an eye
out for discrimination in the industry. "I think women still have a
tough time for several different reasons. Number one, because it's
still a very conservative industry. Some of the smarter employers
have discovered that women do garner a fair amount of press, but I
think many people still look at women as being a difficult situation.
And for the woman herself, if she's planning on having a family, it's
really tough to have kids and integrate them during your career. I've
done it, but if you look at the number of women winemakers out
there, there are not that many. And then if you look at the number
of winemakers with kids, it's a very low number. You can't really
leave. It's not like other jobs where you take some time off, you have
kids, you come back. Winemaking is too responsible of a position.
A lot of the companies are relatively small, so you don't have multi-
ple winemakers at most of them. If you leave, you quit."

Merry, who is married and has two sons, was fortunate enough to
have open-minded employers early in her career. Her first position
as a winemaker was at Mount Eden Vineyards in the Santa Cruz
Mountains. She later became the founding winemaker at Matanzas
Creek Winery in Sonoma County. The owners took no issue when
she brought her son to work every day. "I went back to work when
my oldest boy was three weeks old. He was strapped to me in a
Snuggly every day. He would have to come to the winery with me,
because I was never done at five P.M." As he got older, Merry recalls

from her days as winemaker at Laurier Winery, "I had a crew of ten men, and they would call me 'dude mom' because of the ten-year-old I had hanging around with me all the time!"

As any mother can attest, bringing balanced, happy kids into the world is no easy task, but doing it while trying to create balanced, delicious wines is that much more difficult. It's like raising two kinds of children.

Her oldest is twenty-five and, after finding his way in the world, is now pondering the family business. "Our business is growing, and I think he's getting more interested in it. I think that for a while he thought, 'This is mom's little thing.' And now that I have ten employees and we're building a winery, I think he is starting to pay more attention, but he has never caught the bug. He is a photographer now. He does a few events for me and takes photos for our Web site, and he loves wine. He has a good palate—he learned that growing up! But I just think, who knows. He is only twenty-five. I hadn't even gone back to school until I was twenty-five to become a winemaker."

Merry's second pregnancy, however, resulted in a far greater challenge, the unimaginable kind that most parents spend nine months feeling anxious about. "My eighteen-year-old is a severely disabled child. He had a stroke in utero—it was a very rare thing. He has cerebral palsy, and he is blind and has seizure disorders. Basically, he needs full-time, complete care." When Merry speaks of her youngest son, she is still her matter-of-fact, open-book self, but you can feel a restraint—the kind that comes only from a loving parent who has had to live through something painful and incredibly difficult. It makes her success in the industry that much more awe-inspiring.

Flying Solo

Now Merry is running her own show, but the hours are still grueling at times, and she continues to juggle her life and work to keep a balance. "When you're an owner-winemaker, you've got a lot going on. But there are very few winemakers who don't work long hours all year long. There are very few winemakers who have an eight-to-five job. I can't even imagine. There is no way you can get it done! It's hard for people to understand the supply and demand process that goes on in this industry, compared to something like the tech business, because you can't just make more now. Everything requires so much forethought and planning."

And then there's the fact that she runs the whole show at her own vineyards and winery with the assistance of her husband, Ken Coopersmith. "I love the vineyard part. I especially love the fact that we have our own vineyards now, and we can create the wine from the ground up. That's so rewarding.

"I got here at nine A.M. today, and until twelve-thirty I was tasting with my assistant. We taste every morning at certain times of the year, and that is really exhausting work because it requires so much

---

*M*erry has a great exercise for you to try if you want to learn more about the aromas and flavors of pinot noir: "I find a simple pinot and pour it into glasses. Then I add a different component to each glass that is classic to pinot, like chocolate or cocoa, mushrooms, cola, Bing cherry juice, and maybe some vanilla to give people the flavor of the oak. I put watch glasses (small glass lids from a laboratory supply house) on the top of the glasses to contain the aroma and then let people smell them. I make the additions in pretty big doses so it's obvious even to an inexperienced taster. They don't have a hard time at all; you don't have to go searching for it. It just jumps out."

---

close attention. We taste wines from each vineyard, from each block within the vineyard, and perhaps a unique treatment or experiment on that block. I also taste every individual barrel, some six hundred each year, then I put the blends together a barrel at a time. It takes a phenomenal amount of concentration. I think that's one thing that people maybe misconceive about the tasting aspect and blending—it's one of the most challenging parts of the job, but it's also the most rewarding."

Part of the reward is seeing people get turned on to wine. "I enjoy interacting with our customers. They're so sweet. They get so excited. I'll be here late at night and somebody will call and I say, 'Hi, this is Merry, Merry Edwards Wines,' and they say, 'Merry, you mean *the* Merry? There's a Merry behind the name? There's a person?'"

Quite a person indeed.

11

KIMBERLEE NICHOLLS
Winemaker, Markham Vineyards

Fear is the beginning of wisdom.

—Eugénie de Guérin, *Letters of Eugénie de Guérin*, 1865

YOU'VE HEARD THIS OLD PIECE OF ADVICE A MILLION AND one times: in order to get over your fear about something, you just need to face it. Of course, it's true, but when it comes to wine intimidation, I'd like to add one more step to that tried-and-true process—have a conversation with Kimberlee Nicholls, the winemaker for Markham Vineyards in the Napa Valley.

It's not that Kimberlee has some kind of magic trick to bestow on you, imparting everything there is to know about wine. It's better. She's completely candid and open when talking about her own fears and insecurities on the topic—and she's a winemaker. One of her most comforting anecdotes comes from her first job as a lab technician at Stag's Leap Winery.

"On the day that I left—and I think any time anyone leaves a job and goes to another, there's always that last little minute where you're like, 'Oh my gosh, what am I doing?'—the winemaker at Stag's Leap at the time, John Gibson, put his hand on my shoulder and said, 'Kimberlee, trust your palate. It's better than you think it is.' Coming from someone who is a winemaker and is telling you that, it's what everyone needs to hear, because no one ever thinks that they're good at wine." Apparently, not even a promising young winemaker. This is probably why she takes great joy in helping others who don't quite trust their own instincts to simply, as she might say, get over it!

"I think that people get really hung up, they feel inadequate, because wine has always been perceived as being this real luxury item. In fact, you can enjoy wine for not very much money. And while certain people think that they're really good wine tasters, everyone is so hung up that they have to exactly know what it is. You're like, 'Is that cherry, or is it raspberry, or is it blackberry?' A lot of that comes from your vineyard source. You've got this vineyard that's really high in strawberry and this one that's really high in raspberry. You blend the two together and you've got strawberries and raspberries. And sometimes, you know, they just turn into berries!

"I hear questions like, 'How do you get merlot to taste like merlot and cabernet to taste like cabernet?' Of course, it's a different grape, so I always use the apple analogy. You have different types of apples. You have Gravensteins and you have pippins and you have Fujis and Yellow Delicious—and grapes are the same. They all taste a little bit different. I think that's the easiest way for people to understand, because when you read about it, it just doesn't get right to the point, which is that it's just a variety of a piece of fruit. And that totally makes sense to people."

Now, at every opportunity, Kimberlee tries to do what John Gibson did for her: help others to trust their palates.

"Opening those doors, I love to do that. A hazard of being in the position of a winemaker is that I can be a little bit geeky," she laughs, "but when I'm out and talking about wine, I love being able to tell someone something that just makes the light come on or to

Kimberlee Nicholls

*T*ake a tip from Kimberlee, a great winemaker: "What I really love is sauvignon blanc, and I didn't used to because it could be slightly herbaceous in characteristic, with green bean, asparagus—those kinds of aromas. But sauvignon blanc is such a wonderful wine that pairs well with not only ethnic cuisines like Thai food that have a little bit of spice and heat, but it also does well with all sorts of appetizers and finger foods."

give them a little nugget of information that they can take somewhere else and feel strong and confident about. When I'm out on the road, certainly I want to sell my wine, but it's more important for me just to encourage people to have the food and wine experience together. Don't have what I like; have what you like. That's what's important. If you have what you like, then you can further develop your own palate."

Even though her wines have won awards and kudos from the *San Francisco Chronicle* and *Saveur* magazine, she's never above breaking things down for the novice. Clearly, it's one of her favorite parts of the job. That may well be because Kim isn't the kind of woman who forgets where she came from. There was a time when wine was as much a mystery to her as it is for so many others today.

When Kim was growing up, her family barely touched wine, and she certainly didn't plan to go into the world of vino at all. Her journey to the vineyard started on the most unlikely path of all—one that led from the dentist's chair.

Finding Her Way to Napa

"I was going to go to dental school," she laughs. "I had an uncle who was a dentist, and he was just someone I really admired. His whole lifestyle seemed interesting to me. My dream was to go to the same college he did, and then I was going to move back up to Seattle and work with him in his practice. I decided that that was what I was going to do."

Unfortunately, before Kim even began her freshman year, her uncle passed away from cancer. It was a huge blow. Once she got to school, the difficulty of the program coupled with the loss of her mentor was bewildering. "I had a very good idea of the sciences as they were, but I was fairly traumatized by how difficult it was. School had always been very easy for me, but college was very difficult."

She was unsure of her future plans, but fate played a hand in her young life, aiming her right at wine country.

"I had met my husband when I was going to college in Oregon. Although we were dating, we decided that we were going to make a go of it. He actually is from the wine country, so we moved [to California]."

With no other ideas for her impending future, Kim stuck to a slightly revised version of her original plan. "We were living down in San Jose, and I thought, Well, I'll work for a dentist, and then maybe after I work for a dentist for a little while, I'll go on to hygienist school. So I tried it for a little while—and decided that I just couldn't do it. It wasn't about not being a dentist. For me, it's more about control; I feel like I need to be in charge of what I'm doing and what's going on. I wouldn't have been happy being anything less than a dentist. And since I wasn't willing to go back to school and put my whole heart into it, I needed to find something else I could put my whole heart into, something where I could be in charge of what was going on."

That's when she and her husband sat down to brainstorm about her fuzzy future, and he gave her the encouraging nudge that she needed. "My husband's family is from Sonoma County. He asked me, 'Why don't you study marine biology or something like that?' And I said, 'Yeah, but I don't like to be cold and wet. That's why I moved from Washington State!' So he asked, 'Well, how about the wine industry? There's so much going on there.' That's really what was the impetus for it. When I got into the wine industry, I found it so fascinating that there was so much learning to do. I felt like I was in school, because you learn so many new things almost on a daily basis. Even though I'm making the same product, it's always new—everything changes."

From Gopher to Grape Maven

With her science background, Kimberlee landed a job at Stag's Leap working in the lab. "In the beginning, my average day revolved around pulling a lot of samples and dealing with the enologist, who was in charge of the laboratory, and the winemaker, and getting them wines that they needed to taste to put together blends. I was a gopher—a lab technician is a gopher."

Although she jokes about the job, a glorified errand runner with a fancier title, there was a lot more to the job than that. "I would also do the analysis. In the wine industry, there's a lot of chemistry that goes on, and for me, being a person who truly was not excited by chemistry in college, it was interesting to see whether chemistry can be practical. When you can apply it to something, it makes it much easier to be interested in.

"At the same time, I developed my wine vocabulary, because you are certainly exposed to all of the wines in the winery. And I was just building a confidence for the whole understanding of how the wine-making process works, because, honestly, I knew nothing about winemaking!"

She also didn't have the benefit of growing up around the industry. "I've learned about wine on the job. Certainly, I wish I would have grown up around here so that I might have gone to U.C. Davis or Fresno, or a school that specifically teaches you more about wine and fermentation science. The only thing difficult about it is it takes you a lot longer to develop your connections and relationships when you don't have it as a background. If you have a question, you're like, 'Wow, I just tasted this wine, but I don't know who to

*M*any women find that when they are pregnant, their senses of taste and smell are affected in less-than-desirable ways. For a winemaker, though, it can be an occupational hazard. "Being pregnant really messes with your palate," says Kimberlee. "For me, wine just tasted very acidic—almost metallic. It was almost like having a piece of tin foil or something in my mouth. But my aroma, my sensory perception? When you're pregnant, it is just on fire! You can smell someone smoking a cigarette from twenty buildings away." Kim found that sharpening other senses helped her through the requisite tastings a winemaker must perform. "I made myself concentrate. I'd think, Texturally, how does it feel in your mouth? Does it feel like it's thin? Does it feel like it's not coating your whole mouth? Is it just going on your tongue and coming down the middle? It just forced me to further evaluate how I taste. And I think it made me a better taster, because normally I would just put the wine in and gurgle, gurgle, gurgle, spit."

ask about it,' or 'I'm having this problem.' You don't know who to ask until your network builds."

Nowadays, Kimberlee does trust her own palate, as do many other people who are fans of her merlots, sauvignon blancs, and cabernets. "I think certainly when you put your wines out into the greater public, that is the hardest part, because not everyone likes your wine all the time—it's kind of like someone rejecting your children! You try not to take it personally, because, quite frankly, I think everyone, whether they admit it or not, wants to be liked by everyone else all of the time. You just try to take great pride in what you're doing. Everyone has their own critics. Mine just might be a little more obvious."

Critics aside, Kimberlee tries to keep her focus on the end product and the true recipient of it. "I'm making wine for the consumer, and I hope that I'm making the wines that I like all of the time. I taste them with the winery as a group, so that we all agree on them. It's a very female thing, to work as a team; I think that everyone here at the winery—my associate winemaker and my cellar master and my enologist—we all have great palates. And if we don't all agree, well, maybe I'm just coming down with a cold and I don't know it yet."

Maybe because Kimberlee started out in this business with no compass to guide her, perhaps she's simply an amazing and humble person, but Kimberlee exudes a rare generosity of spirit, especially for someone who's responsible for clinking glasses all over the country. "I definitely feel like winemaking is a collaborative effort. I find it very difficult when people go, 'You made this wine!' I usually say, 'Well, I have a great staff and we all work together,' because it's not just me. I honestly feel more like I am the orchestra leader, or the conductor, who orchestrates this collaboration of events." Whatever she wants to call it, it's certainly beautiful music.

12

STEPHANIE GALLO
Director of marketing, Gallo Family Vineyards

True originality consists not in a new manner, but in a new vision.
—Edith Wharton

THE LAST NAMES OF AMERICANS WHO HAVE ACHIEVED international fame and success can carry about the same clout here as the monarchy does on the other side of the Atlantic. They're our own version of American royalty. But when we sit and ponder the lives of the self-made rich and famous, it's almost a matter of course to assume that no matter how rough-and-tumble their beginnings, their offspring have it oh so easy. And some of them certainly do (as, for example, a certain jet-setting hotel heiress). But then again, there are as many mirror-opposites to the latter example as there are hardworking, rags-to-riches tales dotting their way from east to west.

Take Stephanie Gallo, for instance.

"Every member of our family starts in an entry-level job and has to work their way through. I call it reverse nepotism," she says, laughing.

This is the thing about Stephanie—for being part of the third generation of young Gallos to take over the family's business (reported to earn $1.4 billion in sales yearly and yet, shockingly, still be family owned and operated), she has a way of taking it all in stride, with her humor, dignity, and love for her immediate and extended family safely intact.

When you speak with the Gallos (or, certainly, the two amazing women I talked with for this book, Stephanie and her cousin Gina; see chapter 6), there's an unmistakable evenness about them. It's not exactly humility, because they are indeed proud of their work and the work of their grandfathers, Ernest and Julio. But just as those two young brothers had nothing handed to them, and they leaned on and supported each other from the day the winery started in 1933, so does the rest of the family to this day.

"In order to understand where we're going," Stephanie wisely intones, "sometimes I think it's important to understand where we came from."

This is one of the many strengths that thirty-five-year-old Stephanie has: perspective. It's a useful attribute, considering that her job is all about promoting, sustaining, and creating the winery's image. "I'm the director of marketing for what we call the Domestic Popular category, which includes the domestic popular brands Turning Leaf, Redwood Creek, and Barefoot. In addition to that, I'm responsible for the marketing of the Gallo Family Vineyards brand."

To attain this position, though, Stephanie—whose grandfather is the ninety-seven-year-old patriarch Ernest—had to prove herself worthy of the name on her birth certificate.

"I knew when I was in college that I wanted to get into marketing. My dad said that everyone in our marketing department has previous work experience in some capacity. And for the most part, they have M.B.A.s. He said, 'I can't put you in the marketing department because you're not qualified. I need you, first and foremost, to sell the product. It's probably one of the most challenging jobs that you'll ever have, but you're going to learn the most

Stephanie Gallo

about yourself—how to deal with rejection and how to overcome rejection.'"

After earning her undergraduate degree with honors from Notre Dame, Stephanie left the security of her family's sunny farm in Modesto and dove into the workforce of blustery Chicago, landing a sales position at a local wine distributorship company (and meeting her husband along the way). "It was absolutely invaluable. I probably grew the most in such a short period during my time in sales. It's tough, but I think that's how you begin to add value by having firsthand experience interacting with consumers and customers. Also, when you're down at that street level, you can start spotting trends."

With a few years of sales under her belt, and an M.B.A. from the J. L. Kellogg Graduate School of Management, Stephanie was ready to go back to her family and present herself as an eligible candidate for the family business, starting as an associate marketing manager and eventually climbing her way up to the director-level marketing position she holds now. And she's not alone—her brothers, Ernest and Joe, also had to work their way up the company ladder. There are a total of eleven third-generation cousins all working together in the family business.

So, do they fight? "You know what's funny? We don't. If you talk to my dad, he says that he's never once argued with my uncle. I think that it's a misconception about a family business. You always

---

*W*hat's Stephanie's favorite wine? "I like them all; it's like children. Each one is different, and they all have different personalities. And it depends on my mood and what I'm having. I like the unexpected pairings. For example, I like our Laguna Ranch chardonnay with a steak. It's a pretty heavy chardonnay; it's very rich. It can hold up."

---

hear about modeling behavior, and everyone who is involved with the business currently has worked side-by-side with their grandfather and their father in some way. You see how much respect Ernest had for Julio and how much respect Julio had for Ernest. My grandfather [Ernest] would always say, 'You cannot do it alone.' Our company was built on teamwork, and it was an equal partnership. We don't argue because I think that there is always a way to work it out. Everyone has their own specialties, right? We don't get in each other's crawl space."

Behind Every Great Wine . . .

If you're in the wine business, the wild card of change is something you always need to be ready for, good or bad. The Gallos have certainly been through a lot of it: the fickle taste of consumers, the sudden and sad death of Julio, and the birth of Stephanie's daughter—a fourth generation of Gallos. Just as you can't really predict how grapes will be from one year to the next, you can't see into the future and know quite how life will change, either.

An important and heartening change that Stephanie and her cousin Gina have been happy to witness is how more and more women are becoming visible in the wine industry. "It's changed. I'll give you an example. When I started in sales in 1994, I think most of the hundred-person sales force were men. Now? When I go address our sales organization, the entry-level salespeople, probably now they are fifty to sixty percent women. And the team in Modesto, the winemakers whom I work with, I would say that it is probably forty percent women at the assistant winemaker level. If I look at our marketing department, the majority are women. Our chief technology officer, a pretty big job—she's a woman!"

Stephanie is quick to point out, though, that in the family business, the Gallo women have long played pivotal roles in the gargantuan success of the company.

"This is just a generalization, but I would argue that when I look at the history of our company, my grandmother Amelia did so much for it. My grandmother always took pride that she was the first 'secretary' of our organization. She would drive up to get the licensing; she delayed having a family; she was definitely very active. It's funny, because I think that in every family business the spouse is very active and very involved, but more in a behind-the-scenes role. What was interesting about my mom, Ofelia, was that when she married my dad, she was actually one of our spokespeople. We had a brand called Madria Madria Sangria, and she was spokeswoman for that brand."

Again, these are glimpses of that even, balanced quality that Stephanie Gallo exudes. She is a woman in a responsible position at one of the world's largest wine companies, learning from one of the two giants who started it all. ("He continues to advise today at ninety-seven years old and he has a tremendous sense of perspective—it's amazing," she says of her grandpa Ernest.) As she said earlier, however, she's not one to forget how she got where she is.

"I look at my mom and what she does, and I look at what my aunts have done, and it's definitely not at the forefront; it's a lot of behind-the-scenes work that got done. I don't think that we would be the company we are today if it wasn't for the women who have been involved."

Eye of the Beholder

It's interesting that one of Stephanie's greatest challenges has been her good family name—as it pertains to the bottles, anyway. Just as outsiders have preconceived notions of what it's like to grow up in a famous family like the Gallos, so are there misconceptions about what the family product actually is nowadays. When so much of California's wine industry seems to be turning to boutique wines (that is, smaller wineries creating special—and sometimes very expensive—products), it's no small task to win the confidence of an often-dubious public, especially when it comes to a topic as broad (and that draws such strong opinions) as vino.

"There is this perception that if you produce something in large quantities, then it doesn't equal great quality," she says, alluding to the Gallos' past. Back in the day, Gallo wines were synonymous with jug bottles of Carlo Rossi; Gallo was not known for producing especially fine and carefully crafted wines. Interestingly, though, Gallo's products have indeed kept up with the times.

"In talking to consumers and even some of the young adults, what they're looking for, frankly, is great value. That's the quest. It's

---

*S*tephanie likes to make her own discoveries, too. And when it comes to music, movies, or books, there's no single genre you can pigeonhole her into. "I like to draw inspiration from many different genres, depending on my mood. I have eclectic tastes. It's like the desert island question: if you were on a desert island, what one movie would you want to have with you? I don't know what it would be! It would be everything from *Star Wars* to *Pulp Fiction*. I don't have a favorite-favorite. In music, it's the same. On my iPod, it's everything from Madonna to Yo-Yo Ma to Gwen Stefani. And I'm the type of girl who has three books at her bedside. I just read a chapter and kind of switch around. On my bedside stand right now is Malcolm Gladwell's *Blink*. I really like reading autobiographies that have more of a fictional twist. I just read one on Elizabeth I. Now I'm reading one on Cleopatra. Then I have this other book, which my dad gave me, which is not really about how to raise children, but it's how children model your values."

---

kind of, what is the best value out there? It's cool to be in the know. 'Hey, look at this wine; it costs five dollars, it costs seven dollars, it costs nine dollars. Look what I discovered!' It's what I call the savvy shopper."

Still, shifting old perceptions can feel a little bit like building the pyramids. How do you alter what billions of people potentially think? "It's very hard, but I think the good news is that it can be done. It's expensive and it requires a lot of time. But I guess that's one of the benefits of being in a family-owned business. All of the shareholders are family, and you always have a long-term perspective when you do manage your own business. For us, we're committed to it, and we know that it's the right thing to do for future generations. Frankly, it's what my grandfather and great-uncle always wanted. We want to make their vision real. I think what we're really trying to do across the board—and this is really what my great-uncle and grandfather did—is just to democratize wine; to make wine more accessible for all."

In the end, Ernest and Julio's early wines were arguably more Italian in spirit than they were an icon of Big American Business. Those old jug wines sat on the tables of many an Italian immigrant and working-class, first-generation Italians who weren't willing to give up certain rituals due to high prices.

"I think that what's interesting is my grandfather always had a very simple way to evaluate whether or not it was great wine, or whether or not we made a great wine: Can you drink a couple glasses of it? At the end of an event, do others finish it or just sip it? That's something that I always have in the back of my mind."

Learning at the Table

Even though she certainly had the option not to go into the family business, in some ways there was a stronger pull for Stephanie that went beyond destiny or fate. True, when you talk to her or her cousin Gina, it's easy to see how life on a vineyard could get under your skin. But maybe one of the most important factors that shaped her adult choices in life was the respect she always felt around the table.

"I think that it was so much a part of our life. I think that when you speak with Gina, her experience is the same. When you grow up in a family business, you're exposed to it at such an early age. My parents exposed us in discussions on a regular basis. For example, my dad was involved in sales, as well as in the marketing aspect of it in many ways, and he'd ask my opinion on evaluating television commercials for the wine. He'd say, 'What do you think of it as an advertising perspective?' I was probably thirteen, fourteen, fifteen years old."

And then there was the wine itself. "When I graduated from college and even when I went to grad school, our parents always encouraged us to pursue our dreams, whatever they might be. It's a huge debate—nurture versus nature—but I always think that if I wasn't exposed to it at an early age, what would I be doing? I don't know what else I would be doing. I interviewed at other companies, but I wasn't necessarily as passionate about the product as I would be about wine."

Since the arrival of Stephanie's own daughter, Amelia, the lessons she learned around the dinner table are taking on a new resonance, kind of like a wine when it's peaking at the perfect moment of maturity. "I don't know how you would describe it," she says. "It's just wisdom. Those are the gifts: the insights, the wisdom, and the perspective. I get that every day. I guess the difference is that maybe it's taken me thirty-four years to realize that those are gifts. I think a lot of people don't realize how much our elders can impart their wisdom to us.

"Recently, my grandmother on my mom's side—she's ninety-two and she helps take care of my daughter during the day—she recently wrote my daughter a card for her first birthday, talking about how my daughter made her feel during this last year. She and my grandfather had been married for sixty-eight years, but they'd been together for seventy. She was depressed when he passed away two years ago, and my daughter and my niece have really transformed her. She has a new purpose in life because of her great-grandchildren. What she said to me was, 'I want you to keep this, because I want Amelia to know that I was alive for her first birthday.'

"And so that, to me, out of everything that I've ever received, that really is the most treasured gift of all."

13

RAMONA NICHOLSON

Owner, Nicholson Ranch Vineyards, and president of Napa/Sonoma chapter of Women for WineSense

I was convinced you can't go home again. Now I know better.
Nothing is more untrue. I know you go back over and
over again, seeking the self you left behind.

—Helen Bevington, *The House Was Quiet and the World Was Calm*

IT HAS BEEN SAID THAT YOU CAN NEVER GO HOME AGAIN, but Ramona Nicholson of Nicholson Ranch doesn't buy it for a minute. Not only did she return with her husband and three children to the 160-acre ranch where she'd spent her childhood riding horses and roaming through the fields full of cows, pigs, and goats, she found a way to turn it into her dream job—as the owner of her very own winery.

"My overriding dream has always been to somehow be able to make the ranch support the family and, of course, to keep the ranch in the family, and to raise my family on the ranch. I mean, that has been my desire from the get-go. Even when I was a little girl, I would dream up schemes of having a barn and stalls or giving horse-back riding lessons or having a flower-growing place. I mean, I have imagined every wild scheme possible."

That was the real goal for Ramona—having the family all together. "The benefit and the true joy and my whole point of doing all this is that I am in the same space as my children." The road back home wasn't exactly straight and narrow, though. Unlike many of the other women interviewed in this book, Ramona didn't go to U.C. Davis or have that epiphany that made her switch her major from anthropology to viticulture. In fact, she didn't even stay in Sonoma—or California, for that matter—to go to school. Ramona went clear across the country, to Princeton University in New Jersey.

"My reasoning was that I could really say California was the best and I wanted to stay in California," she laughs. "My roommates laughed at me. I mean, I was the absolute green, friendly California girl. You know, I would talk to anybody. I went to New York City one time, got lost, and went home with people who just picked me up. And my girlfriends were like, 'You can't do that!'"

Yet while her time on the East Coast was a great experience, in her heart, Ramona always knew she'd return to the ranch her father, Socrates, a court reporter, bought on a whim in 1962. ("He is generally an adventurous, gung-ho guy, but he just wanted a nice place

---

If Ramona's dad's name sounds distinctly Greek to you, that's because it is. But Nicholson—where does that come from? "My grandfather immigrated through Ellis Island," Ramona says. "He was a sixteen-year-old boy. He came in and they said, 'What is your name, kid?' He said, 'Leonidas Nicolacopoulos.' They said, 'Yeah, yeah, you are Louie Nicholson. Get going!' So they changed it right then, just like they did so many other names. I had toyed with changing it back to Nicolacopoulos, but people have a tough enough time spelling Nicholson!"

Ramona Nicholson

to settle down and raise his family, which turned out to be me.")

Despite a degree in anthropology, Ramona came home in 1987 and applied for a job at the Mission Inn and Spa in Sonoma not far from the family homestead. After a while, a friend and colleague realized that Ramona, with her people skills, would do well in human resources, and offered to train her for the job. Ramona loved being in HR, and just as her friend suspected, her friendly nature and skills of diplomacy made her soar in the position. So much so that another friend at a finance and software company stole her away to work for him.

This all sounds about as far away from a vineyard as you could get, but fate indeed nudged Ramona toward her destiny. At the new company, she met her husband, Deepak Gulrajani, a native of Bombay, India, who shared Ramona's strong feelings for family but who loved to travel and had grown up in a big city, not in the country as his wife-to-be had.

"I think when he first met me and started thinking about settling down, he was probably hoping for someone who would be a world traveler, but he pretty quickly figured out that if he was marrying me, he was marrying the land. I routinely joke with him that he would have gotten off so much cheaper if he'd found a girl who wanted jewels and nice cars and nice clothes, because I go to him and I say, 'Oh, sweetie, I need a new tractor! Oh, honey bun, can I please have a new wind machine? You know, it's ten thousand dollars. Oh, let's plant another twenty acres! Oh, let's dig a cave!' I'm really expensive."

Ramona and Deepak got married and tried to think of ways to turn the ranch into something profitable. Ramona considered getting into the wine business, but it seemed too bold a move. "I thought, Well, everybody around me is in the business and I am so new. How will I ever be able to compete?" They toyed with the idea of growing olives for olive oil, but it never quite took off. At one point, the head of the olive oil association said to her, "Why aren't you thinking about grapes?" And that was that.

"Finally, I got over it, and I said, 'You know, I think I'd better start thinking about grapes.' And from the get-go, there was never

In addition to building her own winery from the
ground up, Ramona is also the president of the
Napa/Sonoma chapter of Women for WineSense, a
nonprofit wine-advocacy group with chapters all over
the United States. "We believe that wine enhances life
and can be enjoyed responsibly," Ramona says, "and
we want to encourage that and encourage people to
enjoy wine responsibly. A main thrust of the whole
organization is to mentor and educate and encourage
women to get into the field as well, so that happens
both on an organized level and then certainly on a
networking level."

one person who said, 'Oh, you are nothing but a little girl. You can't
come in and play with the big boys.' Nobody ever said that. It is not
like you can't figure this out. If you are smart enough to study and
ask all the right questions, you can generally make the right decisions, and, by and large, that has held true for me."

When she was five months pregnant with her oldest child, Zander, she quit her human resources job and within the week was
enrolled at Napa Valley College, taking viticulture classes. "It was a
huge leap of faith. And the other kind of funny element of it is that
almost all of my projects I have done while I've been pregnant," she
laughs. "I have three kids. The first child, I was starting the whole
venture and starting to study viticulture. In fact, Zander was due on
December tenth and my final exam was December eleventh. He was
three weeks late, so I, of course, had to take the test!" Just to prove
that no moss was growing under her feet, she went through pregnancy two more times during the building of her new business.

"The second baby was Taylor, and he was born in '97. I was running the vineyard and at that point remodeling the main house.
That was a real bad one because I had a contractor who wasn't very

good, and I swear it was the contractor who put me down on bed rest!" And then came number three: "When we decided to do the winery in 2000, I was already pregnant with Natalie, the third child, who was born in July." At that point, Ramona was ready to stop selling her grapes to others and to start producing her own wine, so she was searching for a winemaker and found one in Thomas Brown. "So here is Thomas Brown, this young, hip winemaker going around with this very pregnant woman, talking about what we are going to do for this harvest and making plans for the cave and the winery, so it was really a hoot. After Natalie was born, I was still meeting with architects and planners and contractors, and I just toted Natalie around through it all."

Ramona wouldn't have had it any other way. "I would be out on the tractor and have a beeper on me, and when it was time to nurse the baby, they would beep me and two minutes later I'd pull up next to the house. I would go in and nurse and play with the baby for a little bit, then give the baby back to the babysitter and go back out and be in the vineyard."

For the kids, who are now ten, eight, and six, the winery seemed like an ideal backdrop, but their misunderstanding of their mom's business sometimes led to amusing confusion. "We live maybe a hundred yards from the winery. We do an occasional special event here, like birthdays and weddings, and the kids will see this and say, 'Can I go to the birthday party?' Because a birthday party to them means cake and a goody bag. It could be a fiftieth birthday party or an eightieth birthday party or something like that, it doesn't matter. I tell them, 'No, you don't get to go to the party,' and they say, 'Well, why not? It's our place!'" Ramona laughs. "And I have to tell them, 'No, we are not invited to the party!'"

Getting Off the Ground

The first few years were about planting, growing, and building the winery and the cave, which was where Ramona would eventually make her wine. "In '96, I put in half of the vineyard—fourteen acres of chardonnay and two acres of merlot. In '97, I put in the other half of the vineyard, another fourteen acres of pinot. My intent was to sell for many years until we could manage to do a winery. In January 2000, my husband and I decided to go for it."

She hired an architect and began the drilling for the cave, and even though this was all new to her, Ramona actually relished starting from a clean slate. "You're not tainted by what everybody else is doing, which is a wonderful thing."

In just a few short years since then, Ramona has turned the family homestead into the source of some of the finest wines around. "They are certainly, first and foremost, wines that we enjoy drinking and are proud of. I use only French barrels and I use only the best corks. We are traditionalists through and through. We are not known for cutting any corners around here."

That ideal seems to be paying off. "So many times, you think that you have got the ability to affect how your business grows, you know, with marketing or articles or advertising. And I try to do all those things, but the reality is it's the one-on-one contact with customers. People come in and get to meet our wonderful staff and taste our wonderful wines, and then they go home and tell someone who might not come until six months later, but it is because somebody else had a good interaction here." Her dad, who still lives on the ranch, is getting a kick out of his daughter's success, too. "He does do a fair amount of bragging at this point," Ramona laughs. "He is one of the best salespeople in the tasting room. He doesn't actually go behind the bar, but he chit-chats with everybody who comes in. It's nice for him to see it being successful and see what we have created."

Now that her life has come full circle, all Ramona has to do to see her past, present, and future is look out her window onto the acres and acres of Nicholson Ranch and mull over what was and what's to come. "I'm still only at five thousand cases a year. My goal is to get to ten thousand cases maybe in the next five years. It's just kind of a slow organic growth, I think. The best part of it all has to be that most of the time it hardly feels like I am working. It just seems like it is a natural way of being. It's a natural part of life, being here on the land with the family and having the winery here—it all seems very seamless and natural for me." And so Ramona has proved everyone wrong. Yes, of course, you can go home again.

14

DR. ANN NOBLE

Creator of the Wine Aroma Wheel,
U.C. Davis professor emerita

Invention is the pleasure you give yourself when
other people's stuff isn't good enough.

—Julie Newmar, actress and inventor

AS I MENTIONED EARLIER, WHEN I EMBARKED ON MY very first interview for this book with Heidi Peterson Barrett, it wouldn't be a stretch to say I was a little intimidated. After all, Robert Parker has given her his highest of accolades. When I actually talked with Heidi, I realized that she's a woman with a job, just like me. She is kind and thoughtful; she loves her job and knows she's good at it, but she keeps her wits about her. Heidi doesn't swagger; she strolls confidently.

So even after talking with all of these phenomenal, talented, lauded women of the vine, I must admit that I was nervous about meeting Dr. Ann Noble.

Why? Open any wine book and you are likely to see her referenced in it. Talk to anyone in the industry, and if they haven't been taught by her, they certainly know who she is. Ann invented the

Wine Aroma Wheel (see chapter 1), possibly the most influential tool ever created in the modern wine world. Oh, and she was one of the most respected professors ever to walk the halls of U.C. Davis's Department of Viticulture and Enology. Would this living legend want to tell me her life story? Talk about her interests? Tell me about her dog? Chat about her favorite varietal? Actually, yes.

While her scientific mind and uncanny ability to identify aromas and tastes are a force to be reckoned with, Ann is full of humor, wonder, and, more than anything, a fondness for her former students that stretches beyond the classroom. She's whimsically named her dog (Pinot Noir) and her cats (Riesling and Zinfandel) after grape varietals. She got married for the first time on her fiftieth birthday to a Swedish musician who is blind but who knows the world as she does—through sense perception and memory.

Call her a pioneer in changing the industry, and she's quick to correct you with her New England practicality. "I influence students," she says, "but we collectively, as a department, greatly influence. The people you really influence are the ones you have listened to at some time. These poor guys, you need to tell them it's okay not to know or give them resources to find out.

"So it's an awful lot of advising, and I knew a lot of the students better than most people, which doesn't mean that other people weren't good teachers. The other thing is if you have kids working in your lab, which I did, the lab requires a huge amount of work. That's something that's really important because by demanding of your students, you're teaching them and valuing them. And in that huge amount of work were all these kids, whom I always called elves—although more recently people have said to me, 'That's not politically correct!'" She laughs. "But they were elves because just like the story with the cobbler, in the morning the elves had fixed all his shoes. There's so much work with setting up sensory evaluation. All the glassware had to be coded, cleaned, and uniformly poured. People ask, 'Did I ever have kids?' No, I had students and I have dogs."

Dr. Ann Noble

From East to West

Ann was born in Texas while her father was in the service, but she spent most of her life in Massachusetts. Her father went to work for the U.S. Postal Service after his time with the military ended. "During the Depression, his father used to walk twenty miles a day to work as a plasterer or a mason. So my dad's idea at that point was, 'I want a permanent job. I'll work for the government.'"

Like so many kids, by the time Ann had grown up and was heading off to college, she had no idea what she wanted to do with her life. On the one hand, she was very creative; on the other, she liked science and excelled at it. Her sister was also interested in science and ended up going into dentistry. (Oddly, her mother was a teetotaler, abstaining completely from alcoholic beverages. Her father liked an occasional glass of spirits.)

"I went to Bates in Lewiston, Maine, for my first two and a half years of college. I transferred to U Mass because I really didn't know what I wanted to do; I liked everything," she admits. "So at U Mass one of the things that I found was the fact that there was the ying and the yang." Her first day at the university she was assigned a roommate who told her about food science. When it came time to choose a major, the choice was almost made for her. "They said, 'Oh, you went to Bates and you had a 3.6? We'll take you!' So I majored in food science."

That experience was something Ann never forgot. "That is always one of the things I say whenever I'm advising people. I tell them, 'It's okay if you don't know what you want to do. It's probably better that you think about it.' It didn't even dawn on me as something I had to think about. Back when I was at Bates, I'd go in for counseling, and they'd say, 'Don't worry about it; you'll go to grad school.' But I did think about it, and it was kind of instantly obvious, even though I hadn't really thought about doing food science at that point."

After getting her B.S. from U Mass, Ann went on to earn her Ph.D. at U Mass as well. ("My Ph.D. supervisor was a wonderful person who always could figure out whether I needed to be patted on the head or kicked in the butt.") Her first job would take her farther north.

"My Ph.D. work focused on the chemistry of a highly unsaturated fatty acid. My first job was in Canada at the University of Guelph in the chemistry and sensory analysis of flavor, such as tomatoes, mechanically deboned chicken meat, and cocktail sauce. Interestingly, I learned something important that I use now and that is, I always listen to my nose. I've always paid attention to aromas since I was a kid, and this is one of the things I teach to all beginning wine tasters."

Ann spent her time there teaching, doing research, and developing all the labs. "When I look back, I think, 'My God, I don't believe I walked into that job like that!' I just did it," she marvels.

She worked with colleagues on discovering why some things smell and taste as they do. "We'd say, 'Why is this cocktail sauce so hot?' Well, the answer is it had less sugar in it and sugar dulls the heat from the capsaicin. And off we'd go with our cocktail sauce. But that was random. I was doing things like studying products such as V8; I'd try it out and then get tomato paste and reconstitute it. The company said, 'Well, why have we got this bitter flavor?' I had a project working on that."

As a grad student she thought she was a scientist, but at her first job she discovered that some perceived her as a woman scientist. She had a master's student whom she advised on his research. Unbeknownst to her, he went behind her back to complain about her to her colleagues. When she returned his edited thesis, he had to restrain himself from slugging her. "And it wasn't like anyone said, 'You're really rude to her. You should apologize.' Instead it was that we should have a third person to monitor our conversations!

"So that's what I was there. There were other women in grad school and at my job. They were just like me; they were scientists. They were married, but it didn't seem to detract from their ability to be scientists in the lab. Anyway, a few other things happened, and I clued in quickly. In contrast to her colleagues in the food science department (where she was the first woman), colleagues in other departments were cool and provided valuable collaborations and friendship.

Meanwhile, U.C. Davis needed a professor in its Department of Viticulture and Enology. Ann applied and got the position, but she found herself hesitating about whether to make such a big move. "My colleagues outside the department said, 'You're crazy! Leave, it's a great opportunity!' So I went to Davis just like that."

At U.C. Davis, though, she found herself in the minority. She was the first woman to work in the Enology Department, and some people were a little taken aback by Ann's tell-it-like-it-is nature. "I remember a faculty person told one of my colleagues once, 'She's never going to get tenure if she swears.' And who are you?" She laughs. "You swear; what's the big deal?"

Ann loved her work, but she started to see that maybe there was a better way of teaching the science of enology. "When I first came, Dr. Amerine was still there. I overlapped him one quarter. I was his glorified teaching assistant. I suppose if I'd had a massive ego, I'd have been pissed off about it. In my case, it was like, 'This is cool, because I don't know anything about wine.'"

Surprised? It's true—prior to working at U.C. Davis, Ann had barely touched the stuff. "That was another little factor. When I was in Canada for the first two and a half years, my best friend was a woman who was a glassblower. Her brother worked for a winery. We'd go out canoeing and have a glass of wine. Another thing, this was when I was at a party once, someone had Rioja. I thought, 'I can't drink this; I'll put a little coke in it and make it sweet.' Not killer sweet, but it just takes the edge off the astringent sensation."

Still, lacking in wine knowledge or not, Ann was undeterred. The wonderful thing she discovered was that wine wasn't that difficult to learn about. She did notice, though, that she didn't agree with the way it was being taught in her department. "I was listening to how Amerine was teaching this. What he was doing was having [the students] go around the room and describe the wine and not giving them any words. Immediately, I realized that that wasn't the way to start teaching." When her colleague did begin to give the students words to describe the wine, Ann found that they weren't very useful. "He had started to talk about words, and if you're looking to 1983 and earlier, he had a lot of really dorky words in there."

Inventing the Wheel

Based on her experience as an assistant in those early days at U.C. Davis, Ann became a collector. Not of wine or wine accoutrements—but of words. "So then I'm getting 'words.' I would have the students come up with a word [for an aroma]. They get their own impression. That way, I was generating tons and tons of terms. So I thought, 'All right, I have all these terms. I'm going to put them together to do something with them, to share them with people.'" And that's when the Wine Aroma Wheel was born.

"I introduced it to the wine industry; I wouldn't claim I invented it, that's for sure. I introduced the descriptive analysis. But that's the basic beginning of the Aroma Wheel." Part of the challenge of creating the Wine Aroma Wheel wasn't just collecting all the data; it was breaking through the general snobbery that used to be more prevalent in the wine world. "It's that attitude that wine should be kept holy so that it is inaccessible [to the masses]. So then I said, 'Screw you!'"

At first, Ann was just photocopying the wheel and giving it out to whoever wanted it. Then two things happened: the demand became overwhelming, and some enterprising minds tried to rip off the idea. "I said, 'Okay, that's fine,' and I just modified it again and copyrighted it in my own name." As time went on, Ann wanted to find a way to make it even more useful to the budding oenophile and enologist alike. "I started making the colored plastic wheels. Those were sold. As long as it was at the university, all the money, if there was any profit, was just going back to my sensory [research]."

What Ann really wanted was to teach people that valuable lesson she learned in grad school: to listen with your nose. "I'm doing this Kindergarten of the Nose. When you send a kid off to kindergarten or preschool, you don't tell them, for instance, 'I want you to guess what color this is.'" How would a kindergartener know the color green if someone who knew better didn't supply the word? Ann says it's the same when you're smelling a wine. For instance, if you don't know what apricot smells like or what floral notes are, you certainly can't detect them in a glass and name them.

"Obviously, some people just work and work and work, but for most people that's not the point. If it's hard, I'll go drink beer, or I'll drink lemonade, or I'll drink gin. If I'm telling you what you are smelling, you're absolutely not learning. But if I'm making you tell me what you smell, you are. It's like making someone say something in a foreign language; it could be a little embarrassing, but if you make it really easy, the chances are they will learn."

Her Kindergarten for the Nose is a fun exercise in sensory perception. "I make these physical standards: pineapple, cloves, vanilla, citrus, and so on. So then people smell them and then they smell a wine. When you do that, you recognize the aromas. They always have an 'Ah-ha!' So it's a lot of fun because they're enthused. You basically put these different substances, the natural flavors, into glasses, and then you have the wines that are going to bring out those aromas."

For Ann, the world is one gigantic sensory exploration—even when it comes to her breakfast beverage. "I don't know about you, but I don't have a coffee vocabulary. I do have a coffee wheel that existed from the International Coffee Organization. But I never use it, so I don't have the words for coffee, and that's exactly like the normal wine consumer."

It makes complete sense. It's like teaching shapes to a child by allowing him to put a square block in a square hole and then saying, "Square!" Except, instead of visual clues, Ann's are aromatic. "I use jug wine and I put in a drop of vanilla extract or whatever it is that it smells like, and I select wines like a sauvignon blanc, a riesling, or a gewürztraminer.

"So instead of the professor coming in and saying, 'This is cabernet!' you really start off from what people smell and what the different influences of the aromas are. You don't say, 'This is a cabernet'; you do the reverse."

Life beyond the Lab

Not too long ago, Ann retired from U.C. Davis, leaving behind her Wine Aroma Wheel and her legacy of "smell, do tell" for future students to ponder in the Enology Department. It seems like this might not have been an easy transition. To say that Ann was a woman who was married to her work is certainly not off base. Retirement, though, has been about finding the balance in life.

"Like I said, my kids were my students; my life was the university. I don't think that's a good thing. In fact, when people say, 'You were an influence on me.' I say, 'Yeah, but it wasn't balanced.' I had friendship and support; I'm in contact with almost all of them, and I have pictures of their kids. In fact, now I'm getting pictures of their grandchildren!"

Part of the balance came in the form of a Swedish musician named Gören Muhlert. She met him in 1992, and one year later, on her fiftieth birthday, they were married. "I wasn't looking, but that's a whole other story. Since I got married, it's been balanced. But I still worked until I retired. He's a musician and he likes to go into his studio, close the door, and concentrate, whether he's composing or practicing or teaching some kid. So I'd be working or he'd be working. The two of us wouldn't even emerge until, God knows, maybe eight o'clock at night. Although sometimes you're hungry at six. Goran and I have separate lives behind our working doors, but when some music groups are over, it is a celebration for all. Before that, when I lived alone, I would drink a diet soda or something because when you live alone, what do I do when I come home from work? Then when you have someone else around, sure, then you have wine."

Ironically, her husband is blind and relies on his other senses in order to see. "I listen to my nose; he listens to his nose and his ears," she says. Although Ann's whole world for most of her adult life has involved using her sense of smell, she's tried on occasion to get a complete sense of what her husband's world is like, too. "You concentrate. It's confidence in yourself. If you were to be blindfolded in your house and you couldn't see any light . . . I've tried a couple of times in my own house, and I bash into a wall. I'm off like twenty degrees!"

So now, she's living her new life, post–U.C. Davis. After she'd spent so many years in a lab, you wouldn't think there'd be many more sensory challenges Ann could take on, but whether it's a blindfold or a cup of coffee, she's still exploring. "It's good to have some specific terms, couched in words that are going to translate well. But I'm retired now; I can think about anything I want."

15

PAULA MOSCHETTI

Winemaker, Frog's Leap

At work, you think of the children you've left at home. At home, you think of the work you've left unfinished. Such a struggle is unleashed within yourself: your heart is rent.

—Golda Meir, in Oriana Fallaci, *L`Europeo*

WHEN JOHN WILLIAMS AND LARRY TURLEY STARTED Frog's Leap in 1981, they were a small mom-and-pop operation that produced only about six hundred cases of sauvignon blanc that year and a few cases of zinfandel for good measure. The next year, they dabbled in cabernet sauvignon and cranked out a few cases of that, too.

Not too long after that, and not too far away, a young woman who would eventually become one of their winemakers came of age in Santa Rosa. But Paula Moschetti wasn't dreaming of a life in the surrounding vineyards.

"You know what's funny? I can't tell you how many bios I read of winemakers, and they talk about growing up in a traditional wine-loving family. They have Italian roots or French roots, and they say,

'Wine was always at our table,' or, 'I grew up on my father's farm and we grew our own grapes.' I am the opposite story. Wine really wasn't at our table. We drank Kool-Aid and milk," she says. "And we didn't have bouillabaisse for dinner! We had chicken noodle soup."

So, this Kool-Aid kid eventually grew up and headed off to college. Even then, wine just wasn't on her radar. Of all things, she wanted to study beer. No, not in the keg-party kind of way— Paula wanted to learn to be a brewmaster. "I actually started at U.C. Davis as a food science major and was interested in the brewing end because, if you remember, in the late '80s, the microbrews were coming on strong. So I did an internship at Coors. I wanted to be a brewer. I grew up in Santa Rosa, which is in the Sonoma wine region, but that was really before there was this celebrity status attached to wine. I think it was yet to be discovered what a truly great wine region it was. It was just sort of coming on the scene."

Something funny happened on the way to the brewery, though: Paula was derailed by wine. "I actually had a potential job lined up at a microbrewery the year I graduated. I was waiting for the job to open up, and it didn't. They were still completing construction on the facility."

With her U.C. Davis degree in hand, Paula needed a job. Having grown up in the Sonoma wine region, she thought, I could always fall back on a winery, work in the lab, be a chemist. Do something like that until this job I want opens up. That's just what she did.

"I started at harvest time at Beaulieu Vineyard as a chemist. I really liked it. I was intrigued. I wouldn't say that all of a sudden I had a newfound passion for winemaking. It was an introduction, and it was a wonderful introduction. Over the years, though, it kind of got under my skin a little bit. And I started to fall in love with it."

The difference between making beer and making wine, Paula

Paula Moschetti

*A*lthough Paula's family didn't start out as big
wine drinkers, her dad is one of her biggest fans
now. "My family mostly lives in Santa Rosa. I have
three sisters and a brother. Not all of them are wine
drinkers, but my oldest sister really enjoys wine, and
my dad loves it. He drinks wine every day. He used
to love the Charles Krug wine in the early '70s, so he
would have wine from time to time at the table.
Now he loves the fact that I'm a winemaker, and he's
definitely one of our biggest consumers and attributes his longevity and good health to having that
glass of wine every day!"

says, is that a brewer essentially wants her beer to be the same.
"You have a recipe, and keep quality consistent from brew to
brew. And also, you're a little bit farther removed from the raw
materials you buy, like your barley and your grains." Wine,
though, was much different—and those differences were exciting
to Paula.

"Wine is so connected to agriculture. You're growing something,
and making something from the product that grew. What nature
tended and grew out of the ground is magically transformed into
this wonderful beverage. It's a cool thing, because it's complete. It's
carrying it all the way through, from start to finish."

By 1994, the large-scale production and lab work at BV began to
feel limiting to Paula. She wanted to learn more. It seemed that the
only way to do this was to find a smaller vineyard where she could
do it all. That's when she discovered Frog's Leap.

"Coming over to Frog's Leap as an enologist gave me great experience in all aspects of winemaking, not just in quality management

and the things I was doing at BV. It was wonderful, just being able to be out there on the crush pad and feeding fruit through the crusher, washing a tank, shoveling a tank of skins, setting up the lab, and working on all the environmental programs and the safety programs." Even though the company's production had leaped from those initial six hundred or so cases to forty thousand by the time that Paula joined them in 1994, the place still allowed her to be involved in every aspect of the winemaking process. "I had my hand in everything. Frog's Leap had and still has a very family-owned feeling, very grass roots."

That suited her well. So well, in fact, that she's been with Frog's Leap ever since. "I think, from getting such a wonderful, complete exposure from start to finish of winemaking, under the tutelage of John Williams, the owner and director of winemaking, my passion really started to grow. And I couldn't imagine doing anything else! This is truly a unique lifestyle."

Finding Her Balance

Paula's first surprise in life was discovering that she had a passion for wine. Her second was yet another unexpected path she stumbled upon, one that would become even more important to her than anything else in the world—being a parent to now two-year-old Juliette.

"I have to say that this is truly the passion of my life; hands down the best thing that's ever happened. It's funny because my daughter was a surprise. I really wasn't thinking that I was very maternal. I was always sort of, oh, if it happens, great; if it doesn't, whatever; either way is fine. But you don't know how amazing it is until you experience it. This is my most important job, raising a child, and I am really enjoying it."

Yet even having one child is not without its own stresses, as any parent knows. "It's a little difficult, because my husband runs his own business, and he works crazy hours, oftentimes sixty to seventy hours a week. He roasts coffee, imports espresso machines, and builds coffee businesses for people. My daughter is in daycare, which works for now. My own mother stayed at home, so I sometimes wonder if this is the right choice. I think, 'I have to get up and go to work, and in a sense, so does my daughter!' But Juliette really enjoys preschool, and even when I pick her up after a long day, she doesn't want to leave."

Part of the difficulty is Paula second-guessing her choices, thinking that maybe, like her own mom, she ought to be staying at home with her daughter and that by working full time, she's not doing a good enough job as a parent. "I worry that I should be staying home with her. Perhaps the stay-at-home moms sometimes feel that they should work outside the home. We should feel supportive of one another, have camaraderie, as we are all in this together. There's guilt on both sides. It's part of motherhood, I suppose."

Then there's the difficulty of trying to fit in other things that she used to do before the birth of her daughter and of trying to keep all the balls up in the air. "I'd like to get back to the gym, but if I go after work, then I would have take Juliette from daycare and put her in the gym daycare; then I'd get home at eight or eight-thirty, and that makes for a very long day for my daughter.

"And then there are the trade organizations and the professional organizations. Oftentimes, there are dinners and things like that after work, and that's a little difficult. I know that it's good for me to go for the networking, information, and support, but it's really hard to get motivated to go to a dinner at six o'clock and not get home until ten when you haven't seen your kid all day. I don't know how other women do it. I sort of feel like, for me, I can put my professional life on hold because Juliette's childhood is going to go so quickly. I can wait for that other stuff for four or five years."

The challenges didn't just start after Juliette was born. For any woman winemaker, being pregnant on the job isn't necessarily a walk in the park (or, more fittingly, through the vineyard). "When I had her, she actually came at the end of January, a month early, but that's sort of a good time. I worked a little bit from home when we were in the middle of our sauvignon blanc bottling, which I'd scheduled so that I would be able to have her right when we finished and we'd get that project under our belts. I think the best time to have your baby, if you're a winemaker, is probably December. That's the slowest month."

The calendar may have been cooperating with Paula, but her senses most certainly weren't. "It was really hard for me to taste wine at the beginning. Red wines tasted very metallic to me, and I haven't heard that about all winemakers. There are winemakers who can taste, but for whatever reason mine was limited." Paula could taste certain things, and others would go haywire on her palate. Champagne, for instance, was okay. She reasons that this is because it is a highly acidic wine, and that seemed to do just fine on her tongue.

But reds? "Red wines were very hard for me. And, obviously, you're not drinking when you're pregnant! You're evaluating the wine and you're spitting it out, but it was really hard for me."

Breaking the Mold

Although Paula loves the hard physical work that goes into her job and the deep connection of the soil to the final product, she's never felt pressure to be one of the guys. She is quite the opposite. "You can have other interests that don't necessarily jibe with the whole agricultural lifestyle. Granted, I can't really wear stiletto heels to work or anything. It's all gravel out here and it's wet, cold pavement. I have to wear practical stuff to work, like the Dansko clogs, because you're on your feet, or hiking boots when you're in the vineyard. But I love cashmere, so I always wear cashmere in the winter. And, you know, everybody's got Sevens and Joes, so I'm really into wearing a lot of the nice jeans like that, which fit really well. I just dress casually."

When Paula sees some of the images of women winemakers in the media in general, it seems to her that a particular look is often chosen, and she's happy when she sees a little more diversity image-wise. "Maybe it is because the wine industry in this country is still relatively young, and the pastoral ideal of wine country—acres and acres of vineyards, sage and lavender growing wild along the sides of the road in Napa, and the rural winemakers in the pictures getting ready to dig in to a long day's work—is the one most often used in advertising and media, but is is really great when you get to see other images," Paula says. "You often just hear about the career part, the science part. You don't usually get to hear that these women actually have diverse lives; that they may be a cyclist or a person who crochets. You do hear a lot about women winemakers who really love to cook because the media often talks about food with wine. But it's really funny, because in our family my husband does all the cooking! That's not necessarily one of my strong points, I guess."

At her present job, though, Paula feels that there is great diversity among her peers at Frog's Leap. "There is a great mix of women and men who work at Frog's Leap. There's that great sense of camaraderie here. And we talk about family, friends, television shows, and this and that," she says, laughing. "It is funny how people don't expect that you can be working in an agricultural field and still enjoy putting on makeup."

Paula wants the world outside of the wine industry to realize this, too: that wine isn't a man's sport or a pastime for only one type of woman or one type of person, for that matter—it's for everyone. "I'd really love to see wine as part of a lifestyle, wine as part of meals, imaged more in media, because you're seeing it more now in TV shows and cooking shows and things like that. The

*I*f Paula hadn't taken a job as a winemaker, she may well have ended up as Anna Wintour's right-hand woman with her great love of fashion. "I love Michael Kors, and Chanel and Yves St. Laurent for French fashion. I love Louis Vuitton; I have my share of Louis Vuittons! And I love a lot of the Italian designers. Everybody loves Prada, right? *Sex and the City* was our absolute Sunday night ritual, and I loved just to look at all the fashions—the Jimmy Choo shoes! Before I had a child, I was investing in that sort of thing. Now that I have Juliette, I definitely like to find the fun bargains. I'm not really spending money on that stuff anymore."

younger generation, twenty-one to thirty, is drinking wine more. And I've always been an advocate for exposure of wine targeted specifically to women buyers, like food and lifestyle articles with wine in them in magazines like *Vogue* or *Marie Claire*; these are publications that I read! I love reading about fashion and celebrities. I'm a real girl who just also happens to love wine and the whole process of making it."

This is really essential for Paula. Keeping a balanced outlook on life helps her to be as passionate about her job as she is about the rest of the things that make up her world. To her, it's vital. "Wine is a wonderful part of my life, but it's not my whole life. I have lots of interests, and wine is a wonderful part of it."

She's proud of being a woman in the wine industry, though—make no mistake. "There are women who do start in the lab and who have transcended that. I don't know if that's as much of a pressure anymore, but I definitely felt that when I was first starting out.

And I still feel that it's male dominated, especially in the key positions with more exposure at the bigger, more corporate wineries. But I also feel that women are coming on strong. In this generation, I think that more than fifty percent of the graduates from the U.C. Davis program are women."

Back to the Land

As organic as she may feel just being herself on the job, Paula has stuck around at Frog's Leap for more important reasons than that. The winery is entirely sustainable, and all the vineyards are farmed organically. "It's what we believe," she says. "We know that it not only produces better quality wine, but it just makes sense for the quality of life for employees; it makes sense for giving back to society, in terms of sustainability of the environment. Like everybody says, 'Respect where the grapes are grown.' We try to optimize that, but also not to take wine too seriously. We want to make great, world-class wine, but with a sense of humor; a little tongue-in cheek attitude. And I think people really respond to that."

In 1994, Frog's Leap had outgrown its original spot, the Frog Farm, just north of St. Helena, and John Williams's partner, Larry Turley, wanted to start a new label. It was then that owner and winemaker Williams had the fortunate opportunity to purchase a historic red barn in the heart of Rutherford that used to be a winery back in the 1800s. He was committed to restoring the barn and bring back its winemaking days. With a production of sixty thousand cases a year, Frog's Leap is certainly flourishing at this new site.

"It's a beautiful, old ghost winery," Paula says. "And we're solar powered now. We're still practicing a low-impact form of winemaking; we're not real high-tech. Some people are using that technology, and that's great, but it's not our philosophy. We're really just trying to guide the wine along its way and trying to nudge it in the right direction."

Yet even in that mellow, bucolic atmosphere, at certain times of year that gentle nudging feels more like critical mass. Like during harvest, for instance. "It's actually the most fun time of year, because it's so full of promise, but it's challenging. It's like the fruit is a new-born baby."

As in any parent-child relationship, you're never really sure who your child will grow up to be. In Paula's mind, a big part of dealing with the uncertain nature of a crop comes from staying at Frog's Leap as long as she has. Although it's common practice for wine-makers to hop around from winery to winery every few years, Paula's choice to stay on for twelve years has given her tremendous insight into the grapes they grow. As she says, it takes a while to get to know a winery's own fruit, to see how it's going to be expressed in the final wine. She's also grown very attached to the rhythms of the winery.

"There's the cyclical nature of winemaking that really gets you in touch with it. There's always sort of a memory attached to each vintage. When I'm drinking wines in the bottle from other vintages, I can always remember and reflect back. What was I doing in my life back then? What happened during harvest at that time? Was

---

What are some of Paula's favorite pairings? "I think our sauvignon blanc goes well with oysters, or perhaps a fish with a good lemony caper sauce. It pairs wonderfully, because our sauvignon blanc is very crisp and pure. It doesn't see any wood, it's all stainless steel, so it's pure sauvignon flavor. It's gooseberry and lemongrass and citrus, clean and bone dry. Our zinfandel is really zesty, with raspberry jam [flavors] and a really nice element of cinnamon and spice. It pairs really, really wonderfully with barbecue—anything barbecued!"

---

that when Todd broke the paddle in the crusher? Was that the harvest when we had the really good crush lunches? There was always something going on, and it's really a wonderful way to tie in past memories to what's going on in my life today."

Getting the wine into the bottle can be the most stressful point in the cycle, though, filled with long hours and long days. Paula is pretty philosophical about it. "That's sort of the time that you send your baby off to college, and then that's it! You did what you could do.

"But that's when the fun begins, because that's when the wine can change, grow, and develop. Some mysterious things happen that just make wine very dynamic. It's always something different when you come back to it. Every time you taste it, it's a new experience."

In many ways, Napa's wine country is like her own Walden Pond. Traveling to work each day, Paula continually finds herself in awe of her surroundings. "I just marvel at the utter beauty. It could be in the dead of winter, with the vines dormant and pruned, clouds overhead. It's just beautiful. Or it could be in the springtime when they're just budding out or flowering in bloom. Or it could be after harvest, when the leaves are starting to turn colors. There's just stunning beauty at any given time. And I appreciate it, and I thank God."

When it comes to her colleagues in the industry, she sounds like a kid enthusing about the great friends she made at summer camp instead of a winemaker discussing the professionals who make up the country's most important vineyards. "In Napa Valley, with a few exceptions, people are very open about what they're doing and are willing to share what makes their wine unique or what they are doing in the cellar or in the vineyard. There's not that sense of competitiveness; we all have our own unique take on what we're doing.

"And that's what's wonderful about wine, I think. It's that we all have a place here, and there's a tremendous feeling of camaraderie and sharing. Anything that can improve quality overall helps us all. There is a place for different styles and different wines, because wine has charm, and each has its own personality." Kind of like Paula.

16

LEE MIYAMURA
Winemaker, Meridian Vineyards

Wine could become a place rather than a beverage.

—Morgan Llywelyn, *Bard*

FOR SOME WINEMAKERS, THE PATHS TO THEIR JOBS ARE more direct than for others. A childhood spent in one of California's numerous and fertile grape-growing spots, parents in the business, a summer job in a vineyard, and a straight shot to U.C. Davis all add up to a preordained future just waiting to be plucked.

Like several other Women of the Vine, Lee Miyamura did not start out on a straight path to Meridian Vineyards, where today she is its winemaker of white varietals. To arrive at her final destination, Lee zigged and zagged a little bit, following a connect-the-dots trail that led her from Hawaii to Japan to New Orleans to Napa, as well as indulging in a bit of Ping-Pong action within Meridian itself. Yet Lee isn't the type to mind how she got there; she's enjoyed the ride.

Aloha, United States

Lee was born in Honolulu, Hawaii, just like her parents, who were fourth-generation Japanese Americans. When Lee's dad entered the civil service, he and his wife bade farewell to their home state and took Lee and her sister on a series of adventures to exciting locales far and wide. "I am kind of a Navy brat," Lee says. "We lived quite a few places. I've been all over the place. It's been a very positive experience."

When Lee was ten years old, one of her family's first stops was a town an hour south of Tokyo on the island of Honshu in Japan. Her family was so far removed from its Japanese roots that Lee's knowledge of the language was limited at best. "When I was younger, before we went to Japan, my parents often dropped me off at my grandmother's in the morning. She taught me how to do some of the lowercase alphabet." That was the extent of Lee's familiarity with the language.

Still, she embraced the new adventure and learned to speak Japanese in the five years her family spent there. "I rode a train every day for school and stuff like that. I remember playing with the kids in the neighborhood. When I think about it now, I don't know how I ever got around," she laughs. "I think when you are younger, you tend to be more reactive. As you get older, you make it too complicated. Now I believe you think too much about it, like maybe I'll be watching a [Japanese] program on television or something and I am trying to understand. I take too much time trying to translate it into English, trying to understand what they are saying, and then translating it back to Japanese to say it versus just thinking it."

By the time Lee was fifteen, her dad had a new assignment, and the family left Japan for the Crescent City on the mighty Mississippi: New Orleans. "We were there about a year and half," she says. "I was in the band, and I even marched in a Mardi Gras parade. I got to finish my high school there. I graduated from Patrick High, and then we moved to San Diego, and I started college at U.C. San

Lee Miyamura

One of Lee's favorite outlets outside of work is hanging out with her dog. "I have a Lab mix, and she's kind of making me come home and get her outside. I got her from the winery several years back when one of our cellar workers' dogs had puppies. The guy brought them in to work, and, of course, we're all going to fall in love with them! And some of us went home with puppies that day." Right now, her pup has to stay home, but Lee is hoping that Meridian will open up the premises to a little doggie daycare. "There's something welcoming about walking into the tasting room having a dog there. I mean, it just it melts everyone. Dogs are so giving and forgiving."

Diego." It was the second-to-the-last stop on her whirlwind tour of the world, and the one that brought her to where she is today.

Last Stop, Wine Country

Lee's dad was transferred one more time, to the naval installation in Vallejo, but the family settled in Napa. "I ended up transferring to Sonoma County [for school] and majoring in molecular biology and chemistry. I graduated in 1980 and tried to find a job. I thought, Okay, the South Bay has Genentech [a biotechnology company], but all these companies wanted people with master's degrees. I had a lot of doors close because of that. I even said I am willing! A lot of people were really, really reluctant to go to back to school. For somebody who just got out of school and who's ready to go out into the world, it wasn't what you really wanted."

Lee earmarked grad school for the future but meanwhile needed a job to tide her over. "Harvest came along the next year [in 1986], and I moved to L.A. I got an apartment, but at the same time a seasonal position come up as a lab tech with Beringer in St. Helena, and I thought, What the heck? Let's check it out. My job was to come in early in the morning, run all the fermentation checks on all of the wine. It was done within a couple of hours, and then I'd get in and load up the bottling line and do quality issue checks."

Lee loved it. The lab had a fun atmosphere and she met great people, like Laurie Hook, who was working in the lab as an enologist but who would also eventually become a winemaker for Beringer. "I think a lot of women winemakers have gotten their start by working in the lab, working up through that pathway. I think it was very difficult for women to walk right into it as a winemaker."

This was certainly true for Lee because her initial degree hadn't been in enology or viticulture. She wound her way through a series of positions before eventually landing a job as assistant winemaker.

"If I'd had an enology degree, my promotional status would have been different. But I didn't, so it took longer to get to where I am today. I have to say, though, I feel extremely lucky, but a lot of it also has to do with patience on my part."

Meanwhile, in 1988 the Beringer Blass company purchased a

---

*H*aving spent almost twenty years in the Central Coast region, Lee has witnessed firsthand the effect of the movie *Sideways* on the wine industry there. "*Sideways* really brought so much attention to that part of the Central Coast. We're about an hour north of that area of the San Nunez area, but it definitely has affected us, too. Our pinot grape actually did come from Santa Barbara County. There is a carryover in general to the wine industry because it exposed the wine industry to so many more people."

---

four-year-old small but promising winery called Meridian Vineyards (so named for its position between Los Angeles and San Francisco) in the Central Coast town of Paso Robles. Owned by winemaker Chuck Ortman, the winery had started to make waves with its pinot noir and chardonnay, but there was a lot of room for growth—and that's where Lee came one step closer to being a winemaker.

"The Central Coast of California is the best-kept secret," she says. "A quality assurance position came up there at Meridian, and it was a stepping stone. It was one of those things where it was almost a gift."

Finding Her Mentor

When Lee transferred up to Meridian, it was a much smaller company than it is today. The growth was mostly due to the work of winemaker Signe Zoller (chapter 21), the woman who would become Lee's cherished mentor. "Meridian has grown to more than a hundred thousand cases—a lot of that had to do with Signe, actually," Lee says. "Anything that I achieved has a lot to do with her. She is an extraordinary woman."

Lee started off in various labs at Meridian, working under several different winemakers. Under Signe's watchful eye, Lee progressed from lab tech to special lab manager, from special lab manager to enologist, and, finally, from enologist to winemaker. Signe's mentoring is something Lee has never forgotten. "She is an amazingly sharing person. I'm trying to do the same thing now for others."

Signe knew what it was like to be a woman in a job where she was outnumbered by men ten to three. Today, Lee says it has changed a bit. "It's very cyclical," she says, referring to the fact that nowadays the ratio of men to women as winemakers or lab workers has become much more fluid. "What's really interesting is that just looking at our lab here, for a while it was totally dominated by men. Now it's probably got more women. And our winemaking department at one time was all women, too. We had Signe, we had an assistant winemaker, too, we had two enologists, all women. Right now, though, I am the only woman in the department. And when you look at the candidates we have had, they've been mostly men. For both the lab and for winemaking."

Running the Show

After all the zigging and the zagging, Lee is now Meridian's winemaker in charge of its white varietals—a job she loves and never tires of. "When it comes to making the final blending decision, there is a group of six of us who taste together, and we kind of talk about the blend that we are trying to come up with. A lot of it is appellation driven and among Beringer's family of brands, Meridian falls into the premium brand category. A lot of that has to do with the vineyard sourcing; it's what gives each winery its individuality, along with the winemaker having the ability to select different types of barrels, different processing, fermentation certification styles, and so on."

Although Meridian is no longer the tiny boutique winery it was when it began, Lee still feels at home with and thrilled by her job. "The challenge is still exciting to me. We have had a couple of people who worked here and who have actually left us to go back to small wineries, but I think that was just a mismatch."

Even when she steps out of the gray-stone buildings at Meridian and leaves work, wine remains a big passion for Lee. "If we [winemakers] are at a party and there are a bunch of bottles opened, then it's a free for all!" she says, laughing. "I mean, that is the fun thing for me. I love going somewhere where everybody brings a different bottle, and you've got hors d'oeuvres out on the table and you got all these different wines—cabernet, shiraz, sangiovese. You're trying all these new things and, wow, just being blown out of your mind."

When she looks back, though, maybe it's not so odd that she ended up where she is today. The path might not have been direct, but it does seem that her route couldn't have taken her anywhere else.

"My parents were supportive of me—a lot of it was they just were happy that I was finding work," she says, laughing. "You know, because at harvest that first year, Beringer offered me a permanent position."

Maybe, though, her parents knew Lee's vocation long before she did. "They are not wine drinkers. My dad will drink with me occasionally, but my mom tells this story from when we were traveling all over the place. I think it was on our trip to Hong Kong that I began noticing wine. And my mom said, 'Oh, you are such a funny kid,' because we're not from a family that drinks very much at all. It was something that I was eventually going to come back around to. It's a passion—it truly is a passion."

17

MICHELE OSTROVE

Founder and editor-in-chief of Wine Adventure magazine

Passion is what the sun feels for the earth
When harvests ripen into golden birth.

—Ella Wheeler Wilcox, from the poem "The Difference"

THEY SAY, HOW DO YOU MAKE A FORTUNE IN THE WINE business? Start with a larger fortune! If you don't have the passion, it's not worth it to even get into it in the first place," proclaims Michele Ostrove, "and I think you have to have a passion to be in wine." Indeed, she must have it. How else would someone find the chutzpah to start a magazine from the ground up with nothing more than love for the topic and a willing partner?

In July 2005, that's just what Michele did, and it was a brave step. So far, the twenty-first century has not been kind to the magazine industry; at least a half dozen magazines folded in the first few months of 2006. It's not hard to see why: as the topics that many publications center themselves around become more narrow and niche-focused, most magazines can't muster up the readership and the advertising dollars to get off the ground in the first year, let alone for a decade or two. Michele, though, may well have stumbled upon that right-in-front-of-your-nose idea that the rest of the wine and spirits publications seem to have missed: women.

"I think that women want to enjoy wine with friends and lovers, and they want to go out and taste wine with their girlfriends. Go out on tasting trips and so forth. Women just have a different approach to buying wine and looking at wine and drinking wine, and I think that has not been addressed. It's a different focus on lifestyle, and I wanted to take away the point system and rating of wine and not look at wine in such an intimidating, competitive way."

While it's true that all of the major food publications offer wine columns—often written by women, like *Food & Wine*'s cork-popping diva Lettie Teague—the idea of focusing directly on women is sly genius at work. After all, 53 percent of the wine-buying public consists of women. And if women have the money to buy the vino, it stands to reason that many of us wouldn't mind sinking onto the couch with a nice glass of syrah and a fun read on

You might be thinking, "How do you even begin to launch a magazine? How do you get it out there for people to read?" Amazingly, Michele began the process by cold-calling. "I set out one day and went dialing for distributors, and I didn't stop until I found one. I was so convinced that once I got through to the right person, he or she would see the value in this and want to carry it. My goal is to have it be totally recognized. You know, on the news-stands, as a significant player in the wine publication business. I would like to have as many women readers as we can get. My goal is to get a million if I can."

Michele Ostrove

the topic. "I believe that women particularly like to sit down on a couch or in bed and curl up with a magazine. Who wants to spend all of your off hours from work sitting in front of a computer?"

So far, Michele's been right on target, but it didn't start out as a straight shot to the world of wine.

Ink and Grapes

Michele's path to the world of wine and upstart magazines started about three thousand miles from where she now resides in San Diego, California. Born in Maine, Michele eventually settled in Washington, D.C., where she first became interested in wine and even began collecting some in her midtwenties.

"Before I did this, I had been a freelance writer for many years, and particularly a travel writer. That is where I kind of got the idea to do a magazine that combined food, travel, and lifestyle through the lens of wine. It's something that I always wanted to do. In the interim, I became an editor of a trade publication for a couple of years, which was a great training ground for learning how to run a magazine." Back then, however, she had a much different audience than she does now.

"It was totally different because I was writing to a strictly male audience—and now I'm writing to women. So it's a much easier thing to do, I can tell you that! If you can please a bunch of men wearing hardhats and reading your magazine cover to cover, it's easy to write about wine and food and travel and fun things!"

Michele is having a blast, despite the incredibly hard work and occasionally feeling as if she's running on fumes. ("It's the best job I ever had," she says. "What's been keeping us going through kind of difficult times is that we strongly believe that this is the right time for this magazine.") Michele has taken something she loves and combined it with her natural talent, and made it her life's work. Her investigative journalism side adds an offbeat, intriguing dimension to the magazine that wine journals often lack. For instance, she tracked down Olivia Newton-John not only for the cover of the February/March 2006 issue, but for a great interview where the singer-actress talks about one of her favorite topics, Australian wines.

"We've got Deborah Santana in our May issue. With Carlos, her husband, she has made a sparkling wine with Mumm called Santana DVX." Yes, *that* Carlos Santana—it's not exactly your typical wine-snob information, and that's what makes the magazine so much more interesting, entertaining, and, in the end, informative.

"I'll tell you a small truth. We didn't initially think we were going to do a magazine just aimed at women. We were looking for a way to have our passion support us instead of trying to find a way to support our passion. My partner [Lucien Bonnafoux] and I have actually been funding this ourselves. He is French and a photographer and a businessman, and I am a writer and an editor who has kind of cut my teeth on California wine. We had decided that the two of us should try to combine our talents and create something that we could both do together, and this seemed the natural thing because we both had a long-standing interest in wine and food. We were basically on the fence. Our PR person said that targeting women would put us on the map, and she was absolutely right. We have never looked back."

Wine and food pairing is a topic that seems to confuse people even more than wine itself, but here's a sure-fire tip to help you out when you're utterly unsure: two of the easiest pairing wines are pinot noir, which is not as tannic as other reds, and dry riesling. Sweeter rieslings, like a spatlese, are better with spicy foods, as their acidity can stand up to anything and the sweetness counteracts the spice better than any beer can.

Michele and Lucien's brainchild may have started with a niche-marketing bent, but the more Michele thought about it and worked on the content, the more she discovered what separated her magazine from the rest. "If you take the food magazines like *Bon Appetit*, *Gourmet*, and *Food & Wine*, I think they are more recipe-focused than we are. They deal more with the food. There's some travel woven in there—in *Gourmet* I think more than in some of the others—but I look at that as a recipe magazine. We do offer some recipes, but that's not what we're all about. I think that food and wine are being celebrated in this culture in a way that they really have not been before. People are becoming more sophisticated in their tastes. I think that's why chefs and winemakers are getting celebrity status."

What Michele has tuned in to is the difference between the way men and women discuss topics: in this case, wine. "If you talk about wine and winemaking, I believe that women aren't particularly interested in the wine growing conditions or the terroir or the winemakers' philosophies or how many points a wine is rated. I don't believe that women really care about how many bottles they have in their cellars. It's not a bragging-rights kind of thing for women."

Michele had picked up on the basic tenet of all women's magazines—sharing information. "One thing we say is that women share information, whereas men look at it more competitively. It's kind of one-upmanship for them. Women love to share information with each other. And I think, whether you are a woman winemaker or a woman wine taster, you get excited about wine and you want to share that with other people. We share recipes and we share wine. Women love this. They want to know how to give parties. They want to know how to go traveling to wine country and where they should go and where they should stay and what place has the best spas—and that is the kind of stuff we are tackling."

This has been her approach to all the articles in the magazine. One recent issue featured stories such as "Girls Night In!" which gave food, wine, and movie pairing suggestions for a night at home with the gals (for example, *Casablanca* paired with Casbah Carrot

Soup and a zesty, crisp chenin blanc), to interviews with top female winemakers, to how to plan a wedding in California wine country.

"We want to make it fun. We want to make it approachable, friendly. Here is an example. We have a new column that we started in the last issue called 'The Sensual Side,' and the topic is wine and seduction. It takes a really lighthearted look at how you can use wine to seduce your man. That is something that nobody has ever done before! One of our articles actually in the next issue is how women can get the best service in restaurants, if they are alone or if they are with other women. I mean, that is a huge subject all by itself."

Along with the fun stuff, though, Michele has a mission and a message. "I would like to get women to wake up to the wonderful world of wine and expand their horizons a bit. This is a magazine that will empower some women to get out there and to do things. I mean, whoever would have thought you would be talking about wine and seduction? There are so many topics left to tackle, and it's tremendous."

One topic she feels strongly about is inspiring women to learn through exploring. "I think that women tend to rely on their comfort zones with wine. I met somebody a few months ago who would only drink pinot grigio, and there was no way that she was ever going to try anything else because that was her wine. I think that happens a lot, and one of the goals I have with this magazine is to coax women gently out of their comfort zones."

Another way she's doing this is highlighting female leaders of the industry to further demonstrate that women aren't just enjoying the fruits of the vine—they're making it, too. "I am absolutely trying to feature women, and I am going to be featuring more women winemakers as we go forward. I think that women are really leading this industry."

Meanwhile, Michele and her partner have just about forged their way through the first exciting yet tough year of publishing a new magazine. But for Michele, it's not just about survival. She plans to thrive. "It's been a little bit like running a political campaign," she says, "because a lot of it has been getting out there and shaking hands and meeting people and saying, 'Look at my magazine! Let me tell you about our magazine.' We just came back from a vintners' weekend thing in Monterey County where they didn't even know about us yet. And they were really hungry to get their information out because not everybody knows about the great wineries of Monterey County. A lot of what we are doing is just getting out there and spreading our name verbally."

She's logged a lot of miles this year and pulled more than her share of late nights, but so far, the hard work is paying off. "It takes some time to prove yourself as a player on the block. The odds of a publication succeeding are definitely stacked against us, but I really see so much of a need for this. We just believe in it so strongly." And, it seems, she's found an audience that believes in her, too.

18

STEPHANIE PUTNAM

Winemaker, Far Niente

To want to be what one *can* be is purpose in life.

—Cynthia Ozick

IF STEPHANIE PUTNAM WEREN'T SUCH A PETITE WOMAN, she might have ended up in a career where she'd be more likely to say, "Book 'em, Dano," instead of "Crush 'em, Dirk."

"I wanted to be an FBI agent," says Stephanie, the winemaker for Far Niente's estate chardonnays and cabernet sauvignons. "Now they say that it's not true, but when I was about eighteen, I went to D.C. and I read somewhere that there was a height requirement to enter the FBI. And I'd heard it from another source that you had to be five feet two inches, and I'm five feet—on a good hair day."

Even so, Stephanie couldn't shake her dashed government-job dreams, and with good reason. She and her dad had always been close, and she admired him greatly. So much so, that she wanted to work for the same "company" he did. "At about the same time, my

*T*hink being an FBI agent is about as far from a winemaker as you can get? Just look at what Stephanie once aspired to do. "I wanted to be a brain surgeon when I was a kid. But I got to observe an open-heart operation up front. Up close is very different from observing on a TV screen—and I cringe when I see a needle going into someone. So, obviously, that wasn't going to be for me!"

father passed away. My dad worked for the government, but as an IRS agent. I wanted to work for the government because of what my dad had done; I wanted to make him proud of me. But, you know, sitting around, chasing numbers on a computer wasn't what I wanted to do. I was more of an action person, and I thought the FBI would be really cool. So I wanted to do that for about three years."

While Stephanie was trying to figure out what her future would be, she enrolled in U.C. Davis as a political science major since that seemed like a logical career track. Her path veered off in an entirely different direction. "I think, somewhere in the back of my mind, I always knew that I was interested in wine because I grew up with wine. You know, my parents were avid wine collectors, so I grew up drinking wine and tasting it with them. We used to come up to wine country on the weekends when I was a kid. And at home, my grape juice was color coordinated to whatever type of wine they drank. If they were drinking a white wine, I had white Concord grape juice, and if they had red wine, I had normal grape juice. And if they had it decanted, I had my own crystal decanter for my apple juice. It was always in the background."

Once she had enrolled at U.C. Davis, though, that interest shifted from the background to the forefront. "I took the class at

Stephanie Putnam

*W*ant some great wine advice? Listen to
Stephanie: "Other people may intimidate you,
but don't let people tell you what you should like. If
you like white zinfandel, good for you. My whole
family drinks white zinfandel. They love when I
come to a party, because I'll bring other things for
them to try."

Davis and realized that this was something that I could make a
career out of. It was always evolving. It was something that I would
enjoy doing my whole life."

Bottoms Up

After that first viticulture class, Stephanie was hooked, and she
transferred into the famed Department of Viticulture and Enology,
earning a degree in fermentation science in 1991. After graduation,
she immediately landed an internship with Napa's Hess Collection
Winery, starting in the cellar. "I specifically chose an internship that
would focus exclusively on the cellar right after graduation. And for
that job, at that time, it was kind of hard for women to break in to
the cellar because it is a very physically demanding job."

Stephanie has always been the take-action type and loves outdoor
and physically challenging hobbies. (Lately, she's into a form of mar-
tial arts called Haganah, which she says is "basically, Israeli fighting!
It's just down and dirty. And do I ever expect to use it or want to use
it? No. But it's a lot of fun!") One hobby in particular landed her the
job. "I remember calling [the person who interviewed me] and asking, 'Hey, did I get the job?' He looked at my résumé and said, 'Oh,
you're a rock climber! Okay, you can do the job.' So, I basically got
the job because he knew that I was a climber. He was a climber, too,

so I think that he knew I had the physical stamina to work in the cellar. It's long hours, so it's difficult for any person. It doesn't matter what gender you are."

Stephanie so impressed her boss at Hess during her internship that he asked her to stick around when it was over. "I worked in the cellar for about a year and then got my first full-time job as enologist." She was promoted soon thereafter from assistant winemaker to full winemaker, where she helped to create Hess's line of chardonnay, cabernet sauvignon, and syrah. But a decade into it, she felt as if she needed to prove herself again. She didn't feel completely sure of her abilities and wondered whether her promotions had been given to her due to confidence in her work or because it was convenient for the company. She needed to find out for herself, and that's when Far Niente came knocking on her door, in 2001.

"Getting recruited was kind of a peak for me, because I put in ten years at Hess. So there's always that doubt in your mind: are they just giving me the job [of winemaker] because it's cheaper than hiring someone else new? But being recruited was recognition for me that I really, truly had achieved what I wanted to achieve. I guess I needed recognition from another source that I was doing good work."

It wasn't the first time her path had crossed with Far Niente's director of winemaking, Dirk Hampson. "It's ironic, because when I first graduated from Davis, I was offered two jobs in the cellar. One was at Hess and one was at Far Niente. And Dirk, who was winemaker then and is director of winemaking now, offered me the job. I turned it down because Hess paid fifty cents more an hour!" She laughs. "I was like, you know, I've got bills to pay."

It's funny how those things happen in life: the paths we choose and the ones we opt to pass by. When you end up back where you started, though, it's hard not to think that it was meant to be after all. "It was almost like I came full circle. I turned the job down at Far Niente, and ten years later, I decided to take it. At Hess, I was winemaker, but there were several winemakers. Their opinions carried a lot of weight. Now, the ultimate responsibility lies on me. I didn't, per se, have ultimate responsibility at Hess."

All of the new responsibility that she craved took some getting used to—at Far Niente, Stephanie would be in charge of every aspect of winemaking, from the harvest to tasting, to making decisions on blending. "My first crush at Far Niente was a little intimidating. Ultimately I realized, Wow, if I screw it up, you know, I screw it up. You have this illusion of control, but there is Mother Nature, who is basically everything. That was difficult to deal with. Now, you know, I'm just used to it."

Even so, she carries a lot of responsibility on her small frame. "I tend not to get stressed out too much. I kind of balance it. I find if I play hard and try and take a lot of vacations, then my work life, outside of crush and bottling, it's separate. And I just don't allow myself to get sick. It's just not a possibility!" She laughs. "You know, you have to be honest with yourself. If I do get sick and you know it, it is best that I just make myself little notes, so if I have to make a difficult decision that day, then I'll make sure that Dirk is there and he can weigh in. If it's a decision that can be postponed, then I will.

"But I think there are times that it can be extremely stressful, though. Certainly crush, you know, when you're trying to make the wine. And bottling—God, I hate bottling! It's your last chance to have any impact on the wine. There are so many little things that can possibly happen. You know, the equipment can malfunction, or they don't bring you the products when you expect them. It's like a big domino effect. You're this solitary person in the middle, with about twenty dominoes all coming at you from different directions. And they always crash on you. It's a lot of mental stress. It's very exhausting."

Which is the polar opposite of what people think her job is like. "Lots of people believe that it's ultra-glamorous and that all you do all day long is drink. People are like, 'Oh, wow, you're a winemaker,' and I think it's just the glamour and the drinking. It's very odd. People come up and ask me for autographs! And the exposure to all the fabulous dinners is definitely a perk. I'm very spoiled when it comes

*W*hen it comes to favorite pairings, Stephanie goes classic straight down the line. "Well, actually my favorite food pairing is Dolce and blue cheese. It's my absolute favorite." Dolce is a sister winery of Nickel & Nickel, as well as Far Niente. Dolce produces only one product: a golden late-harvest wine with hints of apricot and orange rind that is the perfect accompaniment to pungent blue cheese. Another classic favorite of Stephanie's? "Port and chocolate. I love port—I always have a bottle on hand. And in my fridge, well, of course, you have to have a bottle of chardonnay and a bottle of champagne!"

to that, and the ability to get wine when I need it. I have too much wine! Some people would kill to have too much wine."

Even though she's the winemaker at one of Napa's more high-end wineries, Stephanie still maintains a down-to-earth attitude on the topic. "I think wine is a little bit more accessible now. Sometimes you can take it too seriously, you know? But I think people are getting more comfortable with what they like. Don't let anyone tell you what you should like or that what you like is bad or wrong. If you like it, but it's not an extremely popular or expensive wine, that's okay. If you like the utmost, most expensive wine out there, that's okay, too. Buy what you can afford.

"I think a lot of people tend to buy wine for special occasions. For my twenty-first birthday, I had several bottles of Bordeaux that my parents had set aside specifically for the occasion. They said, 'For Stephanie's twenty-first birthday.' It was special, but they saved it for a particular day. So if you're going to put wine away for special occasions, mark down what that special occasion is."

Stephanie's best piece of advice? That comes from the vantage point of a daughter who knows what it's like to miss someone important in her life—the celebrations in life aren't only the big occasions; they're right here, right now. "Enjoy wine all the time. Don't wait for the right moment because it will never happen. The right moment is always now."

19

LESLIE SBROCCO

Wine writer and author of Wine for Women

In France, wine is thought of as food so necessary
to life that nobody is too poor to go without it.

—Katharine Butler Hathaway, *The Journals and Letters of the Little Locksmith*

OU'D BE ONE LUCKY TEACHER IF YOU HAD THE CHILDREN
of Leslie Sbrocco in your class—instead of getting an apple
on your desk at the end of the day, you might be given a
rare vintage to try instead.

"I always bring my open and leftover wines to people instead of
pouring them down the drain. I brought some to my son's preschool
teacher in a Girl Scout cookie box, and I said, 'There's the sum of
my life right there—open wine bottles in a Girl Scout cookie box!'"
She laughs.

For Leslie, sharing is what it's all about—and it is the impetus for
her award-winning best-seller, *Wine for Women*. "It's all about
sharing. I think that if you look at the setting, women learn the
most about wines from their friends; they get the information
from their friends. And having a friendly, conversational tone and

attitude [in my book] is the way to do it. As a writer, I think some of the biggest compliments I got have been people who said, 'I have been reading your book—it's like you are sitting in my living room talking to me!'"

Since the book came out in 2003, life has been a whirlwind for this married mom of two. In between book tours, hosting the San Francisco-based PBS show *Check, Please! Bay Area*, writing her wine columns for the *San Francisco Chronicle* and Epicurious.com, and contributing to magazines like *O, Glamour*, and *Good Housekeeping*, she's also managed to write a second book, *The Simple & Savvy Wine Guide*. Yet what's more amazing about Leslie is that all of her projects came from her sheer drive to take what she loved and make a living with it.

"I got into wine by reading every book I could find, all of which were fairly boring. It's certainly changing now, but when I first started to learn about wine, oh my God, it was like reading school textbooks!"

Raised in the Midwest, Leslie was introduced to wine by her father, an airline pilot who frequently took the family on adventures. "My father was a wine drinker, so I remember wine being around the house. I remember being in Europe as a kid and getting to sip wine. I mean, wine was definitely a presence."

After college, Leslie decided to move out to California—but not to go to U.C. Davis, the country's preeminent wine school. She thought at the time that she wanted to be a lawyer but quickly figured out that the button-down world of case study wasn't for her. "I was living in San Francisco. My whole life I'd actually been quite involved in theater and things like that, so I thought, Well, let me just play around—I can always go back to law school." This eventually led her to start a small production company, where she wrote and produced training videos for various companies in the state. Meanwhile, she began spending her free time just north of the city, in wine country.

"Because I was living in San Francisco, in proximity to wine country, it just became one of those things—I was hooked. I mean, I was just smitten like so many people in this business are. And so

Leslie Sbrocco

*A*s groundbreaking as Leslie was with her first
book, so she is with her favorite pairings: champagne and potato chips. What else? "I love rosé wine
with a burrito!"

it became this real avocation for me. I spent all my free time taking
wine classes or being in wine groups or going to wine country, and
spending all my money on wine. It was a true, true passion." That's
when the epiphany occurred. "I looked at myself and I said, 'God,
I wonder if I can make money doing something with wine?'"

First, she took her video production skills and approached local
wineries and TV stations about producing specials on wine. Then,
in the mid-1990s, her luck changed. "A friend of mine whom I
knew from being in wine groups is a magazine publisher, and he
had gotten hired by Microsoft to create what they call a city guide
on the Internet. It was called "Sidewalk." I remember fully point
blank going, 'What is the Internet?'" she remarks, laughing. Leslie
became known as the go-to wine producer, building the wine content for what was, at the time, cutting-edge technology. Then luck
smiled on Leslie again.

"Another friend of mine whom I knew through wine circles
worked for the *New York Times* company–owned paper, the *Press
Democratic* in Santa Rosa in Sonoma County. He was working in
New York at the time and said to me, 'Oh, you know that the *Times*
really wants to create a big wine Internet site, and I can't think of
anybody else to do it.' I had an odd combination of skills, knowing
how to write about wine, talk about wine. I was an expert on the
topic, as well as able to build a Web site from scratch."

The site was called winetoday.com and was tremendously successful. Even when the dot.com industry imploded, the *New York
Times* company kept Leslie on as a wine columnist for its own Web
site. Then came the book.

The Birth of a Boy . . . and a Book

"People thought I was crazy when I first got the idea of writing the book," Leslie says. "I mean, I started in 2001 to think about it and write it. It was published in 2003. And then, it certainly wasn't like it is right now with the explosion of interest in women and wine. People thought, Why would you target that market, why would you separate out women and exclude men? I mean, I really remember going out on a total limb, almost freaking out right before the book came out, going, 'People are either going to love this or hate it.'"

Yet she believed in what she was doing, and kept on. She got an agent interested in her idea but figured it would be eons before any editors bit at the book proposal. She couldn't have been more wrong. "I thought, Okay, now I can take a breath. I can have a baby and relax for a little bit because it takes a while to sell a book. It took me a week!" She laughs. "My first son was little and tiny and strapped to my chest, and I was writing constantly for about nine and a half months to get the book in. So I went, Okay, give birth to a baby, give birth to a book!"

*Y*ou'd think that with all of Leslie's years collecting wine and soaking up the wine country culture, she'd be a collector of decanters, bottle openers, or some other wine-related accoutrements. Guess again. "You know what I do collect? I collect Nativity scenes. I have collections from all over, from Chile, Argentina, France. I remember, as a kid, my mother having three or four Nativity scenes. I just adored them and loved to play with them. Every Christmas, I looked forward to having those Nativity scenes out, and I do that with my kids."

Her instincts were correct—not only was there a market for *Wine for Women*, but a big one at that. "I think the explosion of women in the wine industry and women in wine has recently been a focus because of marketing surveys defining that 'Wow, the statistics say women are are the majority of wine consumers. Great. Well, let's start to look at that.' However, I think that people have started to realize this, and they have over the last few years. I certainly don't take credit, but I was one of the first to start to address it.

"I took a respectful and friendly tone, yet an informative one, and I think that the biggest compliment I got was turning the book in to the copy editor, who was the first person besides my editor who actually read the whole book. She had edited very large manuscripts, and she knew a lot about wine. The first thing she said in her copy edit was, 'I learned more about wine from reading your book than I have from any other wine book.'"

The real strength of the book was Leslie's approach. She remembered the snooze-inducing wine books that had been available when she was learning, and that was not the approach she wanted to take. Leslie wanted the book to be fun, to be something that a woman could really relate to and learn from without feeling as if she were taking on a Ph.D. program in viticulture. And that's how the wine wardrobe was born.

"It really started when I sat down to write the chardonnay chapter. I was thinking about how you could describe chardonnay. It's a blank slate; it can be made into all these different styles. And it dawned on me that it's like your basic black. It was like one of those lightbulb things. And I'm, like, Yes, it is! And merlot is like cashmere. I'd described wine in terms of clothing and style before, but it just all came together. And again, I thought, Okay, I am either going to get slammed for this or I'm going to get kudos."

Not only did she get kudos, she got fans. "I got e-mails from groups of women who were starting their own wine-tasting clubs, and they were doing it according to my wine wardrobe concept. So they would do chardonnays and they would all come dressed in black. They would do a sparkling wine tasting and come in sequins and suede. They would do merlot draped in cashmere. I mean, my God, it just put a smile on my face that people would actually do that because they are having fun and they are learning about wine at the same time."

What Leslie instinctively knew was that it's easier—and more fun—to learn about something when real-life examples are used. Especially examples that would resonate with her readers. "It's just giving that little connector, that little piece of something that you can relate to, to make that lightbulb turn on. *Family Circle* magazine actually did a whole eight-page spread. They hired models, and they dressed them in wine—as my wine! It was unbelievable."

She has had a few critics, though. Some wine writers have called Leslie's approach condescending, but she thinks they're missing the point. "It's the antithesis of condescending—it's inclusive. It's embracing. It's empowering, if it's done well and if it is done in an intelligent way. I have done a lot of research because, obviously, I've been tagged as an expert on women and wine. Our brains work differently. I mean, you can go back to the physiological side of things, on how our brains work differently and how we are wired differently. What you want to do is respect that. Understand that it's not, as I say in the book, that we drink pink and sweet wines and men drink red wine—it's anything but! It's not what's in the bottle; it is how we approach what's in the bottle."

Leslie wants to encourage women (and men, too) to explore and embrace wine with the same passion that she does. "I want to celebrate the women of wine and, in a sense, give permission for people to connect and see and explore it more. Why be intimidated? There is no reason for women to continually feel that way. It's just fermented grape juice!" she exclaims. "I do have a saying that I use in my seminars, which is 'Wine is not to fear or revere but to enjoy.' And that is what has bothered me in the past about wine—that people are afraid to order it and say to themselves, 'Oh, my God, I can't,' or, 'Oh, my God, how am I going to say that grape name right? So therefore I am just going to order a beer.'"

Leslie is trying to help women reveal their passion for wine—to get over their insecurity about being "wrong" and realizing that the only wrong thing is to allow yourself to be held back by fear. "And it can be done. It definitely can be done," she says. "I think that old adage of 'Follow your dream and find your passion, and you'll never work a day in your life'—I think that I am a real case study that it can be done."

20

DARICE SPINELLI

Winemaker, Nickel & Nickel

In what other job can a person be inventor, scientist, landscape
gardener, ditch digger, researcher, problem solver, artist, exorcist,
and on top of all that eat one's successes at dinner?

—Dorothy Gilman, *A New Kind of Country*

I FIND THAT IT'S STRESSFUL WHEN THE UNKNOWN HAPPENS.
That's the *most* stressful, because it hits you and you have to
immediately deal with it." When Darice Spinelli, the winemaker of Napa's ambitious Nickel & Nickel says this, you've
got to wonder: what could be more stressful than being the winemaker who's in charge of overseeing twenty-five vineyards? Well,
plenty.

The nearly ten-year-old winery, perched a stone's throw from the
formidable Opus One in an imported 1770s New Hampshire barn,
is an offshoot of its elder sibling, twenty-six-year-old Far Niente, a
successful 36,000-case-per-year winery that makes only Napa Valley
cabernet and chardonnay. The thing about Nickel & Nickel,
though, is that it's one of the rare wineries making only single-
varietal wines. This means that when you pick up a bottle of

*S*till confused about the difference between a single-vineyard wine and a blended wine? Darice offers the best explanation of all: "We like to think of it in terms of music. Think of a blended wine as the entire orchestra coming together to make a beautiful piece of music, whereas a single-vineyard wine is more like the soloist. After the orchestra plays, the soloist comes through in a really clear way. So, with single-vineyard wines what we're trying to do is we're trying to showcase one specific varietal in one specific spot."

Darice's merlot, for example, merlot is all you will find in the bottle—100 percent of one type of grape. There is no blending with other grapes, and there are no grapes from anywhere other than a single vineyard. It's a bit like being a one-trick pony that has to do its one trick twenty-five different ways.

"I have one varietal from one vineyard," Darice says. "I just have twenty-five different lots, and I put each one into the bottle as a unique wine. With single-vineyard wine, it's a lot of pressure during harvest because we have to try to capture everything that we can from the grapes right then. It's actually one of our most crucial points during the production of wine because no mistakes can happen whatsoever. We have to be on top of our game at all times— what one wine requires is not necessarily what another wine requires. Harvest is a wide-open book. It's whatever it takes. At Nickel & Nickel, we have early hours. I usually get in at five forty-five A.M., but we're here as long as we need to be, so I've been here until eleven at night and then come in at three in the morning."

There are also years like 2005, which throw a complete monkey wrench into Darice's winemaking life. "The harvest was very, very large last year. One of the most challenging things that happened

Darice Spinelli

*A*nother thing Darice didn't appreciate until she got older: her mother's made-from-scratch cooking. "The funny thing was that my mom gave us only homemade food. I always brought homemade cookies with me to school, and I used to trade all my homemade cookies for store-bought because who wants homemade cookies?" she says, laughing.

was because the crop was so large. Let's say that I have a ten-ton fermenter. If they come in with fourteen tons, what do I do with the other four tons? I can't take that and blend it with something else, which is the luxury of having a blended wine. What I have to do is what I call burn another tank, which means I have to put that wine into another tank and then I have to keep that and make a great wine out of that vat, even though I may be running out of tanks for other vineyards."

This is not to say that a blended wine is inferior to a wine made completely of one grape, because it certainly is not. Some of the most prestigious bottles coming out of everywhere from Bordeaux to Santa Cruz are a careful blend of varietals; it's just that each presents its own set of complications and trials. Darice Spinelli has never minded a little hard work, though.

"I grew up on four acres here in Napa and, boy, that was a long time ago! Napa wasn't nearly as developed as it is now. I would get up and bottle feed the goats and cows, and go collect the eggs for breakfast and that kind of thing." For Darice's teacher mom and a dad who worked in the aerospace industry, the farm life in Napa was a return to their roots. "I was born in San Diego. My dad is a person who has always liked the country. He grew up on a farm, and so, as San Diego grew, he actually didn't like the feel of the city."

At the age of six, Darice went from suburbs to farmland—a change that suited her just fine. "I'm not a real materialistic person.

I'm actually more of an outdoor person, as you probably gathered from how I grew up."

Although she spent her formative years in America's foremost wine town, Darice didn't immediately look to the local industry for her future plans. "But isn't that how most young people look at things? You know, the closer you are to something, you just don't happen to move in that direction or pursue it? It's like those people who live next to Disneyland and don't ever go."

It took several more years before Darice found her way into the vineyard. "My parents kind of raised us to be jacks of all trades. They never really pushed us in any one direction. They always felt that we would find our own niche." They were right. "I was a typical teenager," Darice says. "I wanted to leave home to go to college, and I went to college not to pursue winemaking but actually to pursue biochemistry. At that point, I was thinking of genetics or robotics or something like that."

Still, none of these career options seemed to hit home with her. Four years later, she found herself with a degree in biology from U.C. Santa Barbara and with the need for a job. As fate would have it, she found one at a winery.

"I started at Inglenook Winery working in the lab and realized that it was really a fun industry and there was a lot to learn. I left

---

*W*hat's the difference between a chardonnay or a cabernet made in California as opposed to France? Let Darice help you out: "There's a big difference between California and French wines. California wines are much more fruit forward. We get a lot more heat here than in France. The French wines actually have beautiful structure. I mean, you get a lot of middle mouth feel and whatnot. It just depends on the style that you prefer."

Inglenook to go to Beaulieu, and then I went to Franciscan. During my seven years at Franciscan, I moved from working in the lab up to being winemaker at Mount Veeder, which was just a little three-thousand-case winery. When I was there, I could actually go out and hike the vineyards. There were only two of us there doing all of the work, so it was very hands on."

Once Darice got a feel for winemaking on a smaller, more concentrated level, there was no turning back, even when the company she worked with at the time tried to point her in a new direction. "I got moved into a different role where I was production winemaker for all of Franciscan, and it became very much more of a desk job: a lot of figuring it out, orchestration, things like that. Less walking the vineyards and hands-on experience with the wines. It was at that time that I decided this isn't the direction for me. You know, you always think, Oh, yeah, I'm getting bigger and better, but it wasn't the direction that I wanted to move toward."

In 1998, the year after Nickel & Nickel opened, Darice heard through her former boss that the year-old winery was looking for a winemaker for the 3,500-case operation. "When a company gets so large, somebody has to hold the reins, and you do that from an office. So that is how I ended up at Nickel & Nickel. I realized that

*I*n this book, we talk a lot about experimenting with and exploring new wines. But what if you want to play it safe? That's okay! Darice tells us, "One of the things that I do is if I'm with a group and they don't want to experiment, then I fall back to certain wineries because, generally, if you find a style that you like from a certain winery, that style is going to be continued from year to year, and I have certain wineries that I prefer that I know do a great job, and so that's what I'll fall back to."

I was moving down a path that I really didn't want to pursue. So when this opportunity came up, I jumped at it right away. When a company is small, then you don't have quite as many people in the whole production and you do get to spend a lot more time really involved with what you're doing."

That's when things clicked for Darice—and she's never looked back. "My job is a little bit of everything. It starts from the beginning, like right now, normally, I'd be out there hiking the vineyards looking for bud break. At certain times of the year, I'll walk the vineyards and watch how each vineyard is progressing, which also gives me ideas as to what I should be looking for at harvest time. At the winery right now, we are preparing for bottling and getting wines ready for bottling, as well as taking care of the '05 vintage. The thing that you have to keep in mind is that we're working with a perishable product. Even as it's going through fermentation, it's constantly changing, so you can't put off anything. You don't get a second chance."

Another thing that Darice loves about her job is connecting with curious oenophiles at the vineyard. "What's really fun is when the public comes through, and we're actually doing something that they can see because then they're asking all kinds of questions. Those are always really fun conversations, because people are very excited about what you are doing." If you really want to hear Darice get excited, though, just let her start talking about tasting and pairing.

Eat, Drink, and Be Educated

"It's just amazing. I think everybody feels this when they have a fabulous wine and food combination, and you just sit there and you relish it. Food has such a medley of different combinations that it still illuminates me every time I sit down and find something new. In fact, recently, I just had our Suscol Ranch merlot with roasted red pepper soup that the Nickel & Nickel chef had made, and it was . . . oh my gosh, it was the eye opener of the evening. So fabulous!"

This is an important thing to note: that even a winemaker, whom you would expect to know it all, is still in for surprises when she sits down at the table. This is something we all can learn from Darice (and from many of the winemakers in this book)—the key to being a true wine connoisseur is never trying to know it all but instead keeping an open mind.

There are a few tricks of the trade, however, and Darice is happy to share them. "It really has a lot to do with the acid, the sweetness, and the overall fruitiness of both your wine and your food. For me, I'm very texture driven. So what I try to do is to recognize in a wine, how much fruit? How much oak as well? Is it very tart and acidic? You're going to find that a certain style of wine pairs better with certain foods. But, you know, it's tough to say whether something just goes with fish, for instance, because a lot depends on what that fish is like—the weight and the oiliness of it, whether it has a cream sauce or whether it has a lemon sauce. Those are all things to take into account. But it kind of comes down to knowing where your grapes are coming from and what style you want."

What about being asked to select wine at dinner? "That puts a lot of pressure on you because you feel like, Oh gosh, I don't want to experiment because I don't want it to be a bad bottle! But you know what? If I'm going to try something new, I'll just preface that and tell everybody at the table, 'Hey, you want to try something new?' It's tough, but you know, one of the reasons I think women are probably good at it is they really focus on what they're tasting and understand what's going on."

Before becoming overwhelmed by a huge wine list, Darice also suggests simply whittling down the choices. "Obviously, if you have five hundred wines on the list, for anybody it's quite a selection. You have to start by narrowing it down. You can always say, 'Okay, well, do you want white or red?' And then you can say, 'Well, do you want a California cab or do you want to go French?' Being educated about those certain areas, appellations, or varietals definitely helps. So there are ways!"

To Darice, the surefire way is just to keep on trying. "The more you taste, the better you get at it. And, you know, the one thing that is really fun about wine is that everybody's palate is different! That's the wonderful thing. I always get asked, 'What's your favorite wine?' and, you know, my favorite wine isn't necessarily going to be the next guy's favorite wine. People need to lose the idea that they're not good tasters and need to say, 'Hey, you know what? It's whatever you like!' That's an important thing, and if people can get past that, then, you know, gosh, the world is out there! There's so many different wines to try."

What are *you* waiting for?

21

SIGNE ZOLLER

Consultant, Zoller Wine Styling, and winemaker

When you get into a tight place, and everything goes against you till
it seems as if you couldn't hold on a minute longer, never give up
then, for that's just the place and time that the tide'll turn.

—Harriet Beecher Stowe

*I*F YOU HAD TOLD SIGNE ZOLLER WHEN SHE WAS A YOUNG
woman that she would become an influential winemaker,
sought after as a consultant and looked up to by many
young, burgeoning female winemakers, she would have said
that you were crazy.

"I was a housewife, so I started out really late [in wine]. Following the '50s and the nuclear family, I had no expectation of a career.
My mother majored in design and had a brief career as a weaver, but
with five children she didn't have much choice but to stay home. I
didn't have that role model of a mother working outside the home,
and I always expected to get married. I went to college with the
expectation that I would find someone and live happily ever after."
She would, but just not exactly the way she expected.

Signe was born in the Bay Area of Northern California. She and her four siblings grew up in Oakland to the wonderful smells of their mother's eclectic, creative cooking. "I was really interested in science and kind of directed [my schooling] that way because Sputnik went up in the middle or late '50s when I was in high school. Anyone who did well in science at all was pushed in that direction; everybody was afraid of the Russians."

She went off to college at U.C. Davis, majoring in animal science. ("That's the wrong major if you love animals because you end up experimenting on them.") Although she worked in animal science labs after graduation from Davis, she fully expected that her life would be about husband and family.

"When I got married, his identity completely subsumed me. I didn't have any ambition other than being a den mother."

Yet things slowly started to change for Signe. The women's movement was finding its momentum in cities small and large all over the country, with progressive spots like San Francisco leading the way. Signe took notice. "I read *The Feminine Mystique* [by Betty Friedan] and started listening to Gloria Steinem, and looking at my future. I had a couple of children, and I was thinking, 'What is going to happen when those kids are gone? Where am I going to be?' Then my husband got involved with another woman, and that really triggered everything."

Signe was at a fork in the road. She had two boys, ages twelve and ten, a crumbling marriage, and the sting of betrayal weighing her down. What seemed like the worst moment, though, led her to the best future.

Initially concerned about the empty-nest syndrome, Signe had planned to go back to Davis potentially to study computer science. Then her old classmate Mary Ann Graf, America's first woman college-trained (U.C. Davis) head winemaker and the founder of Vinquiry (a company that provides high-quality technical service to the wine industry), pointed her in a different direction. "Mary Ann Graf was an inspiration. She was just about my best friend as an undergrad, and she was majoring in enology. We all thought it was

Signe Zoller

the study of insects; we had no idea what she was studying!" Signe laughs at her ignorance of what would become relative to her life's work. "She loved flavors, and she went around and she smelled everything. She was just one of those people who had the most insatiable curiosity, and she became a success. I was inspired by that and also by the creative process of cooking, which I love. Putting flavors together is very similar to winemaking."

Signe entered Davis's Department of Viticulture and Enology, and while this new world opened up to her like buds on a vine, her old world was barely chugging along. "I left my husband for a year when I went back to Davis. Then he decided he didn't want the other woman, and he wanted to try again. So we decided to try again. But by the time I got through grad school and then got a job with Kendall-Jackson, which was very small at the time, I had changed."

During that year, Signe was on her own. "Davis was two hours away. At that point, I think one of my boys was just starting high school. They were about twelve and fourteen. It's hard to leave your friends when you're that age, and they didn't want to leave their friends, so they stayed with their dad. I came back in a year, although I still commuted down to Davis to go to classes for another year. My husband and I stayed together another ten years—probably for five years longer than it should have been."

Back then, Kendall-Jackson—today a huge company producing tens of thousands of bottles of wine every year—was just a tiny little winery. Signe was one of five other employees working for five dollars an hour, but she loved it.

"I completed my master's thesis while I was at K-J and finished my degree there. And I really loved working. I just loved it. I loved everything about the winemaking creative process and all of the different things. There is such a variety in the things you do; you work with equipment, you go to dinners, and you taste with people. I got to work with Jed Steele, who is just a huge winemaking figure. But my husband just became more and more jealous of my job, so we finally did get a divorce."

*I*f you find that wine tastings intimidate you, take a tip from Signe: "This surprised me, but I found this out in grad school. Hardly ever do you go to a tasting with a bunch of wine snobs. Whatever wine you like, that's the right answer; there is no right and wrong. I've been amazed with that. I thought there would be this huge consensus [at tastings] that, 'Oh, yeah, this is definitely the best wine, and this is the second best, and this is the third best.' Hardly ever does it turn out that way, so you don't need to be afraid of expressing what you think. There is no wrong answer."

It was tough even after all that time, getting used to the idea that her marriage was not going to succeed. Suddenly, Signe was on her own. "To me, when I first thought about leaving my husband, the scariest thing was to go to France. I had always heard that the French don't like Americans. One of the first things I did was study French because I had also heard that they won't speak to you in English. It was only when they realized how bad my French was that they spoke English. It's natural for someone to be hesitant to speak another language if they think you might speak theirs better. I didn't have a bad experience in France at all, as long as I was nice to them and gave French a try. I loved France! But it's like once you break down that barrier—what you most fear—all the rest of them are easy to break down."

Men, Women, and Wine

By the time Signe went back to U.C. Davis, it was the early 1980s yet only about 25 percent of the students in her class were women.

"I don't think the percentage in the winemaking community is that high even now," she says. "A lot of [women] get stuck in the lab. Women get categorized in areas like that, and they can't get out."

That five-dollar-an-hour job at Kendall-Jackson turned out to be the mallet that Signe would use to smash the glass ceiling. "When you start in someplace that small, with only a few people, you have to be able to fill in when somebody goes on vacation, so I got an opportunity to do just everything, including running the pumps, driving a forklift, taking care of compliance, running the lab, and all kinds of things."

This experience landed her a job as a winemaker with Meridian Vineyards, where she would stay and influence many young winemakers (like Lee Miyamura in chapter 16). "When you looked at staffing, you didn't find many women in positions of responsibility [in the wine industry]. Farming and winemaking had been a man's world, so I can understand how it got to be that way, at least historically. Traditionally, men have also been the wine collectors and that's part of the reason, too. And then there are also men who are entrepreneurs, ones who are just starting out; a lot of them are very ego driven and have been playing hardball in some other venue. They tend to choose people like themselves. Women are usually more consensus or team-oriented, so we don't fill the bill. I would love to see more women in the business."

When Signe felt like the odd woman out, it often happened at tastings. "Usually, when people met me, they noticed that I poured wine at a tasting. Although a lot of winemakers were pouring, they automatically assumed that I was a PR person or a marketing person. And I finally told our marketing department that they probably wasted a lot of money with me not having a badge that said 'Winemaker'! They spent all this money to send me places, but then people never assumed that I was the winemaker. Universally, when they find out I am the winemaker, there is amazement because they're just not used to it."

For Signe, though, the real difficulties she faced had less to do with gender bias on the job than with overcoming her unhappy

*I*t's hard for Signe to zero in on which varietal is her favorite, but zinfandel tends to be one she gravitates toward. "As far as the styles, I like a young, fruity style. When you talk about different styles of zinfandel, that variety is all over the board. I like the ones that are zesty and have this lively, peppery, raspberry aroma that just leaps out of the glass. I think a lot of the people who make zinfandel pick it ripe and then they leave it on the skin, but I like to get it off the skin and bottle it before the great aromatics turn to chocolate and leather."

home situation. "I think the biggest challenge, in my case, was having a husband who didn't support it at all. My children finally got to the point where they said, 'You need to leave Dad.' Each one of them came to me individually and independently and said, 'We will both expect our wives to work. We will love it if our wives have careers. We don't understand why Dad doesn't want you to do it.' That was such a wonderful thing to hear from them, and I don't know if I could have done it without them. The challenge was my own inertia actually and just getting out of an abusive situation. They are so supportive and so proud of me."

For the Love of Wine

Today, Signe has no regrets. She has spent the second half of her life doing exactly what she loves. Recently, she embarked on a new chapter in her fruitful years—flying solo.

"It was a huge decision to leave Meridian after eleven years because my job was wonderful. During my last year there, I was working with custom crush clients. What I discovered was I loved working with those people. There are some who are just awestruck by the winemaking process. They want to know all about it, even though they don't know a thing, and they want to do it and they want to learn all about it. I want to do that with people."

It's gratifying for her to be in this position now, of being able to pick and choose her work and her clients. Whether she's consulting on a custom crush or reminiscing on her work as a winemaker with companies like Kendall-Jackson and Meridian (where, for both wineries, she is largely credited with creating wines that grew those businesses to the successful levels where they are now), one thing is certain—it's all still exciting to her.

"When I think of the perks, I think of the people I've met and I think of the great food I've eaten through years of winemaking, because winemakers and chefs so often collide in the marketplace. Wine and food are just thought of and seen together. So whenever you're out for an evening, you don't just go to Sizzler when you're in the wine business; you go someplace nice."

It's not just her colleagues whom she enjoys mixing and mingling with. Signe gets a kick out of the clients, too. "People want to know what a winemaker does. They have no idea. I don't think my boys even have an idea what I do day by day! They want to hear about it; they're fascinated. There are lots of decisions winemakers make from grape to bottle that will influence the way a wine tastes and smells."

Occasionally, though, one of the best decisions is to let Mother Nature perform her magic. Signe provides a wonderful example of just such a happy accident. "In the early days of K-J, a winemaker had left some chardonnay that hadn't finished fermenting, so it had a little bit of sugar left in it. At that time, no one was leaving sugar in chardonnay. Jed Steele had just started as winemaker and asked his good friend John Parducci, 'What do you think I should do with this?' The wine had a lot more sugar than most standard wines at that time. The advice was to bottle it as is. It was sweet enough to balance the bitterness. It smelled so great that people were just in love with it. He created a style right there."

As many surprises as there are in the vineyard and the vat, Signe is looking forward to greeting new ones that will surely come her way in the future. "I think it's really going to be fun. I'm going to enjoy being out on my own. Being your own boss, there's a lot to be said for that. It's fun having your own schedule and meeting all the people. What I would like to start out doing is making wine for people using a questionnaire on what kinds of tastes and varietals they like. Eventually, I would like to get them involved in the process."

If only she knew how many people she's involved in the process already.

GLOSSARY OF
WINE TERMS

acid/acidity   All grapes contain some acid, which is also passed on to the wine made from them. Acid is the tart, sharp taste in your mouth when you drink a wine. The acidity level also helps wine to age.

aeration   The term for allowing a wine to "breathe." The wine softens, and the taste is smoother. Aeration also enhances the flavors by opening them up when they mix with oxygen in the air. You can aerate the wine by decanting it or swirling it in your glass.

aftertaste   Describes what you taste after you swallow the wine. It is also referred to as the "finish." It can linger, be harsh, or be short, or you may not experience anything at all. Finer wines usually will have a longer and more complex aftertaste.

appellation   Refers to the specific region where a grape is grown. This system was originally developed by the French and was used to regulate and maintain the authenticity of their wines. It is called the Appellation d'Origine Controlée (AOC) in France.

aroma   The smell of the wine. In wine circles it is often referred to as the "bouquet."

astringent   This is the cause of the "puckery" sensation that can be found in wines that are high in tannins, most often in red wines, although tannins exist to a small degree in whites as well. This effect usually decreases with age. Astringency tends to decline with bottle age or when the bottle is decanted.

balance   Being well balanced is a prized characteristic for wine; it refers to the fact that one component of the wine, such as alcohol, sugar, fruit, tannins, or acid, does not stand out distinctively on the palate. Well balanced is when wine is harmonious in all of its elements.

balthazar   The term used to describe a huge bottle of wine that contains the equivalent of sixteen standard bottles.

barrel fermented   Although white wines are most often fermented in stainless steel tanks, some are fermented in oak barrels in order to increase the complexity and the flavor of the wine. This process results in the flavors and the aromas of spice and vanilla from the wine interacting with the wood. The technique is most often used with chardonnay.

berrylike   An adjective often used to describe red zinfandel wines. It refers to the sweet, fruity, and ripe flavors and aromas of blackberries, raspberries, cranberries, and cherries.

big   Wines that are very intense in their overall rich flavors. A big red wine is often tannic, and big whites can have a higher alcohol content and glycerin (a by-product of fermentation that gives the sweet taste).

blend   The means of mixing different grape varieties, vineyards, regions, or vintages to create a particular wine.

body   The feeling of the weight of the wine in your mouth. Wine is often described as being full-bodied, medium, or light-bodied. It is the effect from the combination of alcohol, glycerin, and sugar, such as described in the definition of "big."

breed   This is reserved for wines that come from the classic grape varieties called "noble grapes." It stands for wines that have reached the most refined levels of balance, aroma, complexity, and structure based on the varietal's character.

brut   A term used when describing champagne or sparkling wine. It indicates that it is a dry wine—drier than extra dry.

cabernet sauvignon   The most popular of the red grape varieties. It can be made as 100 percent of the cabernet varietal and in blends. It is full of flavor and can have hints of blackberry, plum, black currant, and even chocolate or leather.

cave   An underground cellar where wine is stored. It can also be used to describe a temperature-controlled wine storage cabinet installed in your home.

Chablis   A type of white wine named for the region Chablis, an area of France. It is made from chardonnay grapes.

Champagne A region of France that is most popular for making the only sparkling wine that can truly be called champagne. The method to produce this style was invented there as well. It is made from one white grape (chardonnay) and two reds (pinot noir and pinot meunier).

chardonnay This is often considered the most popular of white grapes in the United States. It is a grape that can produce a fruity style or be infused with oak. It is grown all over the world and is very abundant. It can have hints of pineapple, lemon, apple, pear, melon, butter, honey, and butterscotch, depending on the style.

chenin blanc A type of grape that produces a lighter style of wine and has distinctive flavors such as melon, citrus fruits, and peaches. It is semisweet compared to chardonnay or sauvignon blanc.

citrusy This aroma and flavor term is used to describe the hints of citrus fruits most commonly detected in white wines when the grapes were grown in colder regions.

clone The offspring of grapevines containing the genetic makeup of the parent vine. There is a lot of worldwide research in this area, testing how to clone varieties to ripen earlier than other varieties do or to produce more grapes on the vine.

complexity When a wine is rich and deep but is also balanced, it is often described as containing many layers of flavor. Complexity distinguishes a great wine from a good wine.

corked The term used when a wine smells and tastes moldy due to a defective or inadequately sterilized cork. It often smells like wet cardboard.

crisp The term often used to describe white wines with high acidity and possibly even some tartness that is pleasing on the palate.

crush Refers to the season in which North America harvests and crushes its grapes. It usually is in September or October.

decanting A method in which you slowly pour wine from the bottle into a decanter or a carafe to leave the sediment behind. The process is usually used only for red wines.

depth Refers to the complexity of a wine. It is usually reserved to describe a premium wine that has subtle layers of flavor that develop in the mouth.

dry A wine that has very little noticeable sugar.

earthy A term used to describe a wine that has a hint of aromas and flavors such as wet soil or dirt.

enology   The science of winemaking.

fermentation   The natural process in which sugar is converted into alcohol by yeast, thus transforming grape juice into wine.

filtering   This process removes any sediment, grape skins, or dead yeast, and it also clarifies the wine. It is performed after fermentation and before bottling.

finish   A term used to describe the impression that lasts after the wine is swallowed. A long, complex finish is most desirable in good wines.

flight   A systematic approach or theme that is often used in wine tastings where several small portions of wine are poured into three, four, or more glasses in order to establish a particular order to the tasting.

floral   Hints of the taste and the smell of flowers in the wine; usually found in white wines.

fortified   A wine that has a higher than normal alcohol level. The additional alcohol is added to it, bringing the levels up to 16 percent or more.

fruity   The quality of having fresh or cooked fruit flavors and aromas in a wine, such as berries, figs, or apples, and sometimes even extra sweetness.

full-bodied   A wine that gives the impression of filling the mouth, as opposed to being "thin." It usually derives its fullness from a high alcohol content.

fume blanc   The name first coined by Robert Mondavi years ago to refer to sauvignon blanc. Its characteristics are crispness with an herbal or grassy quality.

gewürztraminer   *Gewürz* in German means "spicy." This grape has a spicy flavor to it and gives off a distinctive aroma and flavor. It has floral aromas and usually is dry. This grape can also be late harvested to make a dessert wine.

glycerin/glycerol   A natural by-product of fermentation. It creates the effect of a sweet taste on the tip of the tongue. Higher levels of glycerin are usually found in higher alcohol content wines or those harvested later.

grassy   A term normally used to describe a sauvignon blanc that has hints of grass or vegetal undertones.

herbaceous   The detection of herbs in the taste and the smell of the wine; frequently found as a characteristic of cabernet sauvignon and sauvignon blanc.

jammy   A term most often used to describe California zinfandel wines, referring to the natural berry taste of the grape.

late harvest   Wines made from grapes that are picked from the vine much later than normal. This creates a higher sugar level and is usually done for dessert wines.

legs   This effect is often mistaken for a sign of quality. In fact, it refers to the droplets of wine that form inside and appear to run down the sides of the glass when it is swirled around. It evaluates the amount of alcohol concentration. The higher the alcohol content, the more impressive the legs will look.

length   Measures how long the flavor of the wine lasts in the back of the throat after it has been swallowed. It is used as a synonym for "finish."

maceration   The process of keeping and stirring the grape skins with the juice in order to extract as much as possible of the color, the tannin, and the aroma from the skins during the fermentation process.

magnum   Refers to the bottle size. It holds twice the amount of a standard-size wine bottle and is often given as a gift.

malolactic fermentation   This is a secondary fermentation process that occurs, naturally converting the malic acid (tart) into lactic acid (milky). It makes the wine softer by reducing the acidity. It can create a more complex red wine and is often described as "buttery" in white wines. Not all wines go through this secondary fermentation process.

maturity   When a wine reaches a well-balanced state and is ready to drink.

meritage   A California winery term used to describe a Bordeaux-style blended wine that often doesn't meet minimal labeling requirements for varietals. If a winery produces a meritage, that is usually its most expensive blended dry wine.

merlot   A grape traditionally used to make blends in the Bordeaux region of France. It has been very popular on its own, and its pleasant fruit flavors and low tannins make it very versatile with food.

muscat   A type of grape used for dessert wine or to create a sparkling wine with floral and honey aromas.

nouveau   A tradition started in Beaujolais, France. It indicates that the wine was fermented quickly and is fruity and fresh. It is the first release of the new harvest each year. It is a young but immediately drinkable wine that should be consumed within a few months of its release.

New World   A term used collectively to refer to winemaking countries outside of Europe.

nutty   Wine that has flavors or smells that evoke nuts. It can be described as roasted, toasted, buttery, cashews, almonds, or hazelnuts.

oaky   A wine that derives its flavor and aroma from oak. The flavor is introduced when the wine is in contact with wooden barrels made from oak. New barrels create a much stronger oaky flavor in a wine than older barrels do. Its characteristics can be described as vanilla, toasty, or roasted.

oenophile   A term used to describe a person who appreciates and enjoys fine wine.

off-dry   A wine that is slightly sweet.

Old World   A term used collectively to describe the winemaking countries of Europe.

open-up/opening-up   Some bottled and cellar-aged red wines do not demonstrate their full flavors when the cork is first removed. After a few minutes in a wine goblet and mixing with the air, however, the appearance of many flavors and characteristics can be detected. They can also disappear quickly, as fast as thirty minutes for some wines.

oxidized   Oxygen can be the enemy of wine. Wine can lose its freshness when exposed to the air, causing it to lose flavor and aroma and go out of balance.

palate   A term used as a synonym to "mouth" by wine tasters.

peppery   The term used mostly to describe spicy wines. It is usually detected in white wines such as gewürztraminer or in red wines such as syrah.

petite sirah   A red grape that is a little peppery and spicy. It is grown primarily in California and is a descendant of the Rhone grape, syrah.

pinot blanc   A grape that has good fruit flavor when it is young, and is similar to, but doesn't have as much depth as, a chardonnay.

pinot grigio   A grape that produces a dry, crisp white wine. The French translation for this grape is *pinot gris.*

pinot noir   A classic grape variety found in Burgundy and Champagne in France. Today, many well-made pinot noirs are coming out of California and Oregon, and they will please your palate with soft tannins and cherry and even mushroom flavors.

racking   The traditional method of clarifying wine. The winemaker moves the wine from one container to another to get rid of any sediment or particles. It is like decanting on a very large scale. It is a more laborious process but is much gentler on the wine than filtration, so the wine retains more flavor and aromas.

residual sugar   A measure of the amount of sugar remaining in the wine after the fermentation process. Dry wines have little or no residual sugar, whereas dessert wines have a much higher concentration and thus more alcohol.

rich   Describes a wine that has a full flavor without being sweet. The richness is a result of the alcohol content, the glycerin, and the oak in a dry wine.

riesling   A grape that has a floral aroma and is native to Germany and Alsace, France. It ranges in style from crisp and dry to off-dry, to extremely sweet, and is now found in many different regions, such as California, Oregon, Washington State, and the Finger Lakes in New York. It is one of the most versatile and food-friendly grapes and can produce a very good dessert wine as well.

robust   A full-bodied, intense wine.

round   A wine that is smooth, with no dominating characteristics such as tannins, acid, or glycerin.

sangiovese   A classic Italian grape that winemakers in California are working with to make their own style, now known as Cal-Ital wines. It is a medium to full-bodied wine with flavors of cherry and spice.

sauvignon blanc   A grape that has distinctive acid and herbal flavors. It can often be described as grassy or herbal.

sediment   The solid particles that form in a bottle of wine as it matures.

single vineyard wine   A wine that is produced from the grapes of a single vineyard. These wines do not mix varietals or regions and usually carry the name of the vineyard on the label.

soft   Wines that have a low level of acid can produce a soft texture on the palate. The term can also be used to describe a wine with a low alcohol content.

structure   The overall texture, feel to the palate, and balance of a wine. This is referred to as the complete description of the wine.

sulfites   This is a natural by-product of the fermentation process. All wines contain some level of sulfites, but with today's technology, winemakers are not adding it as they did for decades throughout the history of winemaking. Sulfites kill off bacteria and act as a preservative for the wine.

table wine   Refers to any wine in the United States that contains less than 14 percent alcohol by volume. The label can simply state "table wine" and by law not be required to state the percentage of alcohol in the wine.

tannin   A natural substance that comes from the skins, the seeds, and the stems of the grapes. It is the primary reason for a wine to taste bitter and to produce a "puckery" sensation in the mouth. Tannins are very common in red wines because they are fermented with the skins; white wines generally are not. Tannins can act as a preservative, and age is the most important factor in taming the tannic nature of a wine.

tart   A synonym for the term *acidic*. It is descriptive of underripe fruit.

terroir   A French word to describe the collective characteristics of the vineyard. It includes the soil, the slope, the climate, the drainage, the topography, and other attributes of the growing conditions.

thin   A wine that lacks body and substance; the opposite of full-bodied.

toasty   A descriptive flavor that can be a by-product of aging in oak barrels.

varietal character   The particular flavors and smells produced by a type of grape.

vegetal   A word describing an undesirable aroma or flavor resembling plants or cooked green vegetables, such as green peppers.

viniculture   The science of growing wine grapes.

vinification   The process of wine making, or the craft of growing grapes to make wine.

vintage   Refers to the year the grapes grew and to the wine that was made from those grapes.

vintner   Refers to the wine producer or proprietor of the winery.

viticulture   Refers to the cultivation of grapes, often for use in the production of wine. It is one branch of the science of horticulture.

yeast   A very important microorganism that causes the fermentation process by converting sugar to alcohol.

zinfandel   A red grape that is used to make a robust, spicy, berrylike wine, as well as a semisweet blush wine called white zinfandel.

FURTHER READING

BOOKS

Ewing-Mulligan, Mary, and Ed McCarthy. *Wine Style: Using Your Senses to Explore and Enjoy Wine.* Hoboken, NJ: John Wiley & Sons, 2005.

Le Cordon Bleu. *Le Cordon Bleu Wine Essentials: Professional Secrets to Buying, Storing, Serving, and Drinking Wine.* Hoboken, NJ: John Wiley & Sons, 2001.

McCarthy, Ed, and Mary Ewing-Mulligan. *Wine for Dummies,* 3rd edition. Hoboken, NJ: Wiley Publishing, 2003.

Peynaud, Emile. *Knowing and Making Wine.* Translated by Alan Spencer. New York: John Wiley & Sons, 1984.

Robinson, Andrea Immer. *Andrea Immer Robinson's 2006 Wine Buying Guide for Everyone.* New York: Broadway Books, 2005.

———. *Great Wine Made Simple: Straight Talk from a Master Sommelier.* New York: Broadway Books, 2005.

Sherbert, Felicia. *The Unofficial Guide to Selecting Wine.* Foster City, CA: IDG Books Worldwide, 2000.

WEB SITES

Andrea Robinson
www.andreaimmer.com

California Association of
   Winegrape Growers
www.cawg.org

Court of Master Sommeliers
www.courtofmastersommeliers.org

Divas Uncorked
www.divasuncorked.com

Local Wine Events
www.localwineevents.com

Robert Parker
www.erobertparker.com/info/
   glossary.asp

Janice Robinson
Fine Writing on Fine Wines
www.janicerobinson.com

Leslie Sbrocco
www.lesliesbrocco.com

Vino Wine Dictionary
www.vino.com/guide/wine-term-
   glossary.asp

Wine Adventure Magazine
www.wamagazine.com

Wine & Women
www.womenwine.com

Wine Business Monthly
www.winebusiness.com

Wine.com
www.wine.com

Wine Institute
www.wineinstitute.org

Wine Market Council
www.winemarketcouncil.com

Wine Spectator
www.winespectator.com/Wine/
   Home

Women for WineSense
www.womenforwinesense.org

Women of the Vine
www.womenofthevine.org

Worldwide Wines
www.worldwide-wines.com/
   Glossary.htm

INDEX

Page numbers in *italics* refer to illustrations.